Monologues from Shakespeare's First Folio for Older Men: *The Comedies*

The Applause Shakespeare Monologue Series

T0352791

Other Shakespeare Titles From Applause

Once More unto the Speech Dear Friends
Volume One: The Comedies
Compiled and Edited with Commentary by Neil Freeman

Once More unto the Speech Dear Friends
Volume Two: The Histories
Compiled and Edited with Commentary by Neil Freeman

Once More unto the Speech Dear Friends
Volume Three: The Tragedies
Compiled and Edited with Commentary by Neil Freeman

The Applause First Folio in Modern Type
Prepared and Annotated by Neil Freeman

The Folio Texts
Prepared and Annotated by Neil Freeman, Each of the 36 plays of the
Applause First Folio in Modern Type individually bound

The Applause Shakespeare Library
Plays of Shakespeare Edited for Performance

Soliloquy: The Shakespeare Monologues

Monologues from Shakespeare's First Folio for Older Men:
The Comedies

Compilation and Commentary by
Neil Freeman

Edited by
Paul Sugarman

APPLAUSE
THEATRE & CINEMA BOOKS
Guilford, Connecticut

APPLAUSE
THEATRE & CINEMA BOOKS

An imprint of Globe Pequot, the trade division of
The Rowman & Littlefield Publishing Group, Inc.
4501 Forbes Blvd., Ste. 200
Lanham, MD 20706
www.rowman.com

Distributed by NATIONAL BOOK NETWORK

Library of Congress Cataloging-in-Publication Data available

Library of Congress Control Number: 2021944366

ISBN 978-1-4930-5694-1 (paperback)
ISBN 978-1-4930-5695-8 (ebook)

♾™ The paper used in this publication meets the minimum requirements of
American National Standard for Information Sciences—Permanence of Paper for
Printed Library Materials, ANSI/NISO Z39.48-1992

Dedication

Although Neil Freeman passed to that "undiscovered country" in 2015, his work continues to lead students and actors to a deeper understanding of Shakespeare's plays. With the exception of Shakespeare's words (and my humble foreword), the entirety of the material within these pages is Neil's. May these editions serve as a lasting legacy to a life of dedicated scholarship, and a great passion for Shakespeare.

Contents

FOREWORD

Paul Sugarman

Monologues from Shakespeare's First Folio presents the work of Neil Freeman, longtime champion of Shakespeare's First Folio, whose groundbreaking explorations into how first printings offered insights to the text in rehearsals, stage and in the classroom. This work continued with *Once More Unto the Speech Dear Friends: Monologues from Shakespeare's First Folio with Modern Text Versions for Comparison* where Neil collected over 900 monologues divided between the Comedy, History and Tragedy Published by Applause in three masterful volumes which present the original First Folio text side by side with the modern, edited version of the text. These volumes provide a massive amount of material and information. However both the literary scope, and the literal size of these volumes can be intimidating and overwhelming. This series' intent is to make the work more accessible by taking material from the encyclopediac original volumes and presenting it in an accessible workbook format.

To better focus the work for actors and students the texts are contrasted side by side with introductory notes before and commentary after to aid the exploration of the text. By comparing modern and First Folio printings, Neil points the way to gain new insights into Shakespeare's text. Editors over the centuries have "corrected" and updated the texts to make them "accessible," or "grammatically correct." In doing so they have lost vital clues and information that Shakespeare placed there for his actors. With the texts side by side, you can see where and why editors have made changes and what may have been lost in translation.

In addition to being divided into Histories, Comedies, and Tragedies, the original series further breaks down speeches by the character's designated gender, also indicating speeches appropriate for any gender. Drawing from this example, this series breaks down each original volume into four workbooks: speeches for Women of all ages, Younger Men, Older Men and Any Gender. Gender is naturally fluid for Shakespeare's characters since during his time, ALL of the characters were portrayed by males. Contemporary productions of Shakespeare commonly switch character genders (Prospero has become Prospera), in addition to presenting single gender, reverse gender and gender non-specific productions. There are certainly characters and speeches where the gender is immaterial, hence the inclusion of a volume of speeches for Any Gender. This was something that Neil had indicated in the original volumes; we are merely following his example.

Once More Unto the Speech Dear Friends was a culmination of Neil's dedicated efforts to make the First Folio more accessible and available to readers and to illuminate for actors the many clues within the Folio text, as originally published. The material in this book is drawn from that work and retains Neil's British spelling of words (i.e. capitalisation) and his extensive commentary on each speech. Neil went on to continue this work as a master teacher of Shakespeare with another series of Shakespeare editions, his 'rhythm texts' and the ebook that he published on Apple Books, *The Shakespeare Variations.*

Neil published on his own First Folio editions of the plays in modern type which were the basis the Folio Texts series published by Applause of all 36 plays in the First Folio. These individual editions all have extensive notes on the changes that modern editions had made. This material was then combined to create a complete reproduction of the First Folio in modern type, *The Applause First Folio of Shakespeare in Modern Type.* These editions make the First Folio more accessible than ever before. The examples in this book demonstrate how the clues from the First Folio will give insights to understanding and performing these speeches and why it is a worthwhile endeavour to discover the riches in the First Folio.

PREFACE AND BRIEF BACKGROUND TO THE FIRST FOLIO

There has been an enormous change in theatre organisation recent in the last twenty years. While the major large-scale companies have continued to flourish, many small theatre companies have come into being, leading to

- much doubling
- cross gender casting, with many one time male roles now being played legitimately by/as women in updated time-period productions
- young actors being asked to play leading roles at far earlier points in their careers

All this has meant actors should be able to demonstrate enormous flexibility rather than one limited range/style. In turn, this has meant

- a change in audition expectations
- actors are often expected to show more range than ever before
- often several shorter audition speeches are asked for instead of one or two longer ones
- sometimes the initial auditions are conducted in a shorter amount of time

Thus, to stay at the top of the game, the actor needs more knowledge of what makes the play tick, especially since

- early plays demand a different style from the later ones
- the four genres (comedy, history, tragedy, and the peculiar romances) all have different acting/textual requirements
- parts originally written for the older, more experienced actors again require a different approach from those written for the younger

ones, as the young roles, especially the female ones, were played by young actors extraordinarily skilled in the arts of rhetoric

There's now much more knowledge of how the original quarto and folio texts can add to the rehearsal exploration/acting and directing process as well as to the final performance.

Each speech is made up of four parts

- a background to the speech, placing it in the context of the play, and offering line length and an approximate timing to help you choose what might be right for any auditioning occasion
- a modern text version of the speech, with the sentence structure clearly delineated side by side with
- a folio version of the speech, where modern texts changes to the capitalization, spelling and sentence structure can be plainly seen
- a commentary explaining the differences between the two texts, and in what way the original setting can offer you more information to explore

Thus if they wish, **beginners** can explore just the background and the modern text version of the speech.

An actor experienced in exploring the Folio can make use of the background and the Folio version of the speech

And those wanting to know as many details as possible and how they could help define the deft stepping stones of the arc of the speech can use all four elements on the page.

The First Folio

(FOR LIST OF CURRENT REPRODUCTIONS SEE BIBLIOGRAPHY

The end of 1623 saw the publication of the justifiably famed First Folio (F1). The single volume, published in a run of approximately 1,000 copies at the princely sum of one pound (a tremendous risk, considering that a single play would sell at no more than six pence, one fortieth of F1's price, and that the annual salary of a schoolmaster was only ten pounds), contained thirty-six plays.

The manuscripts from which each F1 play would be printed came from a variety of sources. Some had already been printed. Some came from the playhouse complete with production details. Some had no theatrical input at all, but were handsomely copied out and easy to read. Some were supposedly very messy, complete with first draft scribbles and crossings out. Yet, as Charlton Hinman, the revered dean of First Folio studies describes F1 in the Introduction to the Norton Facsimile:

> It is of inestimable value for what it is, for what it contains. For here are preserved the masterworks of the man universally recognized as our greatest writer; and preserved, as Ben Jonson realized at the time of the original publication, not for an age but for all time.

WHAT DOES F1 REPRESENT?

- texts prepared for actors who rehearsed three days for a new play and one day for one already in the repertoire
- written in a style (rhetoric incorporating debate) so different from ours (grammatical) that many modern alterations based on grammar (or poetry) have done remarkable harm to the rhetorical/debate quality of the original text and thus to interpretations of characters at key moments of stress.
- written for an acting company the core of which steadily grew older, and whose skills and interests changed markedly over twenty years as well as for an audience whose make-up and interests likewise changed as the company grew more experienced

The whole is based upon supposedly the best documents available at the time, collected by men closest to Shakespeare throughout his career, and brought to a single printing house whose errors are now widely understood - far more than those of some of the printing houses that produced the original quartos.

TEXTUAL SOURCES FOR THE AUDITION SPEECHES

Individual modern editions consulted in the preparation of the Modern Text version of the speeches are listed in the Bibliography under the separate headings 'The Complete Works in Compendium Format' and ' The Complete Works in Separate Individual Volumes.' Most of the modern versions of the speeches are a compilation of several of these texts. However, all modern act, scene and/or line numbers refer the reader to The Riverside Shakespeare, in my opinion still the best of the complete works despite the excellent compendiums that have been published since.

The First Folio versions of the speeches are taken from a variety of already published sources, including not only all the texts listed in the 'Photostatted Reproductions in Compendium Format' section of the Bibliography, but also earlier, individually printed volumes, such as the twentieth century editions published under the collective title *The Facsimiles of Plays from The First Folio of Shakespeare* by Faber & Gwyer, and the nineteenth century editions published on behalf of The New Shakespeare Society.

INTRODUCTION

So, congratulations, you've got an audition, and for a Shakespeare play no less.

You've done all your homework, including, hopefully, reading the whole play to see the full range and development of the character.

You've got an idea of the character, the situation in which you/it finds itself (the given circumstance s); what your/its needs are (objectives/ intentions); and what you intend to do about them (action /tactics).

You've looked up all the unusual words in a good dictionary or glossary; you've turned to a well edited modern edition to find out what some of the more obscure references mean.

And those of you who understand metre and rhythm have worked on the poetic values of the speech, and you are word perfect . . .

. . . and yet it's still not working properly and/or you feel there's more to be gleaned from the text , but you're not sure what that something is or how to go about getting at it; in other words, all is not quite right, yet.

THE KEY QUESTION

What text have you been working with - a good modern text or an 'original' text, that is a copy of one of the first printings of the play?

If it's a modern text, no matter how well edited (and there are some splendid single copy editions available, see the Bibliography for further details), despite all the learned information offered, it's not surprising you feel somewhat at a loss, for there is a huge difference between the original printings (the First Folio, and the individual quartos, see

Appendix 1 for further details) and any text prepared after 1700 right up to the most modern of editions. All the post 1700 texts have been tidied-up for the modern reader to ingest silently, revamped according to the rules of correct grammar, syntax and poetry. However the 'originals' were prepared for actors speaking aloud playing characters often in a great deal of emotional and/or intellectual stress, and were set down on paper according to the very flexible rules of rhetoric and a seemingly very cavalier attitude towards the rules of grammar, and syntax, and spelling, and capitalisation, and even poetry.

Unfortunately, because of the grammatical and syntactical standardisation in place by the early 1700's, many of the quirks and oddities of the origin also have been dismissed as 'accidental' - usually as compositor error either in deciphering the original manuscript, falling prey to their own particular idosyncracies, or not having calculated correctly the amount of space needed to set the text. Modern texts dismiss the possibility that these very quirks and oddities may be by Shakespeare, hearing his characters in as much difficulty as poor Peter Quince is in *A Midsummer Night's Dream* (when he, as the Prologue, terrified and struck down by stage fright, makes a huge grammatical hash in introducing his play 'Pyramus and Thisbe' before the aristocracy, whose acceptance or otherwise, can make or break him)

> If we offend, it is with our good will.
> That you should think, we come not to offend,
> But with good will.
>   To show our simple skill,
> That is the true beginning of our end .
> Consider then, we come but in despite.
> We do not come, as minding to content you ,
> Our true intent is.
>   All for your delight
> We are not here.
>   That you should here repent you,

The Actors are at hand; and by their show,
You shall know all, that you are like to know.

(A *Midsummer Night's Dream*)

In many other cases in the complete works what was originally printed is equally 'peculiar,' but, unlike Peter Quince , these peculiarities are usually regularised by most modern texts.

However, this series of volumes is based on the belief - as the following will show - that most of these 'peculiarities' resulted from Shakespeare setting down for his actors the stresses, trials, and tribulations the characters are experiencing as they think and speak, and thus are theatrical gold-dust for the actor, director, scholar, teacher, and general reader alike.

THE FIRST ESSENTIAL DIFFERENCE BETWEEN THE TWO TEXTS

THINKING

A **modern** text can show
- the story line
- your character's conflict with the world at large
- your character's conflict with certain individuals within that world

but because of the very way an 'original' text was set, it can show you all this plus one key extra, the very thing that makes big speeches what they are

- the conflict within the character

WHY?

Any good playwright writes about characters in stressful situations who are often in a state of conflict not only with the world around them and the people in that world, but also within themselves. And you probably know from personal experience that when these conflicts occur people do not necessarily utter the most perfect of grammatical/poetic/ syntactic statements, phrases, or sentences. Joy and delight, pain and sorrow often come sweeping through in the way things are said, in the incoherence of the phrases, the running together of normally disassociated ideas, and even in the sounds of the words themselves.

The tremendous advantage of the period in which Shakespeare was setting his plays down on paper and how they first appeared in print was that when characters were rational and in control of self and situation, their phrasing and sentences (and poetic structure) would appear to be quite normal even to a modern eye - but when things were going wrong, so sentences and phrasing (and poetic structure) would become highly erratic. But the Quince type eccentricities are rarely allowed to stand. Sadly, in tidying, most modern texts usually make the text far too clean, thus setting rationality when none originally existed.

THE SECOND ESSENTIAL DIFFERENCE BETWEEN THE TWO TEXTS
SPEAKING, ARGUING, DEBATING

Having discovered what and how you/your character is thinking is only the first stage of the work - you/it then have to speak aloud, in a society that absolutely loved to speak - and not only speak ideas (content) but to speak entertainingly so as to keep listeners enthralled (and this was especially so when you have little content to offer and have to mask it somehow - think of today 's television adverts and political spin doctors as a parallel and you get the picture). Indeed one of the Elizabethan 'how to win an argument' books was very precise about this - George Puttenham, *The Art of English Poesie* (1589).

A: ELIZABETHAN SCHOOLING

All educated classes could debate/argue at the drop of a hat, for both boys (in 'petty-schools') and girls (by books and tutors) were trained in what was known overall as the art of rhetoric, which itself was split into three parts

- first, how to distinguish the real from false appearances/outward show (think of the three caskets in *The Merchant of Venice* where the language on the gold and silver caskets enticingly, and deceptively, seems to offer hopes of great personal rewards that are dashed when the language is carefully explored, whereas once the apparent threat on the lead casket is carefully analysed the reward therein is the greatest that could be hoped for)
- second, how to frame your argument on one of 'three great grounds'; honour/morality; justice/legality; and, when all else fails, expedience/practicality.
- third, how to order and phrase your argument so winsomely that your audience will vote for you no matter how good the opposition - and there were well over two hundred rules and variations by which winning could be achieved, all of which had to be assimilated before a child's education was considered over and done with.

B: THINKING ON YOUR FEET: I.E. THE QUICK, DEFT , RAPID MODIFICATION OF EACH TINY THOUGHT

The Elizabethan/therefore your character/therefore you were also trained to explore and modify your thoughts as you spoke - never would you see a sentence in its entirety and have it perfectly worked out in your mind before you spoke (unless it was a deliberately written, formal public declaration, as with the Officer of the Court in The Winter' s Tale, reading the charges against Hermione). Thus after uttering your very first phrase, you might expand it, or modify it, deny it, change it, and so on throughout the whole sentence and speech.

Neil Freeman

From the poet Samuel Coleridge Taylor there is a wonderful description of how Shakespeare puts thoughts together like "a serpent twisting and untwisting in its own strength," that is, with one thought springing out of the one previous. Treat each new phrase as a fresh unravelling of the serpent's coil. What is discovered (and therefore said) is only revealed as the old coil/phrase disappears revealing a new coil in its place. The new coil is the new thought. The old coil moves/disappears because the previous phrase is finished with as soon as it is spoken.

C: MODERN APPLICATION

It is very rarely we speak dispassionately in our 'real' lives, after all thoughts give rise to feelings, feelings give rise to thoughts, and we usually speak both together - unless

1/ we're trying very hard for some reason to control ourselves and not give ourselves away

2/ or the volcano of emotions within us is so strong that we cannot control ourselves, and feelings swamp thoughts

3/ and sometimes whether deliberately or unconsciously we colour words according to our feelings; the humanity behind the words so revealed is instantly understandable.

D: HOW THE ORIGINAL TEXTS NATURALLY ENHANCE/ UNDERSCORE THIS CONTROL OR RELEASE

The amazing thing about the way all Elizabethan/early Jacobean texts were first set down (the term used to describe the printed words on the page being 'orthography'), is that it was flexible, it allowed for such variations to be automatically set down without fear of grammatical repercussion.

So if Shakespeare heard Juliet's nurse working hard to try to convince Juliet that the Prince's nephew Juliet is being forced to (bigamously) marry, instead of setting the everyday normal

'O he's a lovely gentleman'

which the modern texts HAVE to set, the first printings were permitted to set

'O hee's a Lovely Gentleman'

suggesting that something might be going on inside the Nurse that causes her to release such excessive extra energy.

E: BE CAREFUL

This needs to be stressed very carefully: the orthography doesn't dictate to you/force you to accept exactly what it means. The orthography simply suggests you might want to explore this moment further or more deeply.

In other words, simply because of the flexibility with which the Elizabethans/Shakespeare could set down on paper what they heard in their minds or wanted their listeners to hear, in addition to all the modern acting necessities of character - situation, objective, intention, action, and tactics the original Shakespeare texts offer pointers to where feelings (either emotional or intellectual, or when combined together as passion, both) are also evident.

SUMMARY

BASIC APPROACH TO THE SPEECHES SHOWN BELOW

(after reading the 'background')

1/ first use the modem version shown in the first column: by doing so you can discover

- the basic plot line of what's happening to the character, and
- the first set of conflicts/obstacles impinging on the character as a result of the situation or actions of other characters
- the supposed grammatical and poetical correctnesses of the speech

2/ then you can explore

- any acting techniques you'd apply to any modem soliloquy, including establishing for the character
- the given circumstances of the scene
- their outward state of being (who they are sociologically, etc.)
- their intentions and objectives
- the resultant action and tactics they decide to pursue

3/ when this is complete, turn to the First Folio version of the text, shown on the facing page: this will help you discover and explore

- the precise thinking and debating process so essential to an understanding of any Shakespeare text
- the moments when the text is NOT grammatically or poetically as correct as the modern texts would have you believe, which will in tum help you recognise
- the moments of conflict and struggle stemming from within the character itself
- the sense of fun and enjoyment the Shakespeare language nearly always offers you no matter how dire the situation

4/ should you wish to further explore even more the differences between the two texts, the commentary that follows discusses how the First Folio has been changed, and what those alterations might mean for the human arc of the speech

NOTES ON HOW THESE SPEECHES ARE SET UP

For each of the speeches the first page will include the Background on the speech and other information including number of lines, approximate timing and who is addressed. Then will follow a spread which shows the modern text version on the left and the First Folio version on the right, followed by a page of Commentary.

PROBABLE TIMING: (shown on the Background page before the speeches begin, set below the number of lines) 0.45 = a forty-five second speech

SYMBOLS & ABBREVIATIONS IN THE COMMENTARY AND TEXT

F: the First Folio

mt.: modern texts

F # followed by a number: the number of the sentence under discussion in the First Folio version of the speech, thus F #7 would refer to the seventh sentence

mt. # followed by a numb er: the number of the sentence under discussion in the modern text version of the speech, thus mt. #5 would refer to the fifth sentence

 # /#, (e.g. 3/7): the first number refers to the number of capital letters in the passage under discussion; the second refers to the number of long spellings therein

within a quotation from the speech: / indicates where one verse line ends and a fresh one starts

[ ] : set around words in both texts when F1 sets one word , mt another

{ } : some minor alteration has been made, in a speech built up, where, a word or phrase will be changed, added, or removed

{†} : this symbol shows where a sizeable part of the text is omitted

TERMS FOUND IN THE COMMENTARY
OVERALL

1/ **orthography**: the capitalization, spellings, punctuation of the First Folio
SIGNS OF IMPORTANT DISCOVERIES/ARGUMENTS WITHIN A FIRST FOLIO SPEECH

2/ **major punctuation**: colons and semicolons: since the Shakespeare texts are based so much on the art of debate and argument, the importance of F1 's major punctuation must not be underestimated, for both the semi-colon (;) and colon (:) mark a moment of importance for the character, either for itself, as a moment of discovery or revelation, or as a key point in a discussion, argument or debate that it wishes to impress upon other characters onstage

as a rule of thumb:

a/ the more frequent colon (:) suggests that whatever the power of the point discovered or argued, the character is not side-tracked and can continue with the argument - as such, the colon can be regarded as a **logical** connection

b/ the far less frequent semicolon (;) suggests that because of the power inherent in the point discovered or argued, the character is side-tracked and momentarily loses the argument and falls back into itself or can only continue the argument with great difficulty - as such, the semicolon should be regarded as an **emotional** connection

3/ **surround phrases**: phrase(s) surrounded by major punctuation, or a combination of major punctuation and the end or beginning of a sentence: thus these phrases seem to be of especial importance for both character and speech, well worth exploring as key to the argument made and /or emotions released

DIALOGUE NOT FOUND IN THE FIRST FOLIO
∞ set where modern texts add dialogue from a quarto text which has not been included in Fl

A LOOSE RULE OF THUMB TO THE THINKING PROCESS OF A FIRST FOLIO CHARACTER

1/ mental discipline/**intellect**: a section where capitals dominate suggests that the intellectual reason ing behind what is being spoken or discovered is of more concern than the personal response beneath it

2/ feelings/**emotions**: a section where long spellings dominate suggests that the personal response to what is being spoken or discovered is of more concern than the intellectual reasoning behind it

3/ **passion**: a section where both long spellings and capitals are present in almost equal proportions suggests that both mind and emotion/feelings are inseparable, and thus the character is speaking passionately

SIGNS OF LESS THAN GRAMMATICAL THINKING WITHIN A FIRST FOLIO SPEECH

1/ **onrush**: sometimes thoughts are coming so fast that several topics are joined together as one long sentence suggesting that the F character's mind is working very quickly, or that his/her emotional state is causing some concern: most mod ern texts split such a sentence into several grammatically correct parts (the opening speech of *As You Like It* is a fine example, where F's long 18 line opening sentence is split into six): while the modern texts' resetting may be syntactically correct, the F moment is nowhere near as calm as the revisions suggest

2/ **fast-link**: sometimes F shows thoughts moving so quickly for a character that the connecting punctuation between disparate topics is merely a comma, suggesting that there is virtually no pause in springing from one idea to the next: unfortunately most modern texts rarely allow this to stand, instead replacing the obviously disturbed comma with a grammatical period, once more creating calm that it seems the original texts never intended to show

FIRST FOLIO SIGNS OF WHEN VERBAL GAME PLAYING HAS TO STOP

1/ **non-embellished:** a section with neither capitals nor long spellings suggests that what is being discovered or spoken is so important to the character that there is no time to guss it up with vocal or mental excesses: an unusual moment of self-control

2/ **short sentence:** coming out of a society where debate was second nature, man y of Shakespeare's characters speak in long sentences in which ideas are stated, explored, redefined and summarized all before moving onto the next idea in the argument, discovery or debate: the longer sentence is the sign of a rhetorically trained mind used to public speaking (oratory), but at times an idea or discovery is so startling or inevitable that length is either unnecessary or impossible to maintain : hence the occasional very important short sentence suggests that there is no time for the niceties of oratorical adornment with which to sugar the pill - verbal games are at an end and now the basic core of the issue must be faced

3/ **monosyllabic:** with English being composed of two strands, the polysyllabic (stemming from French, Italian, Latin and Greek), and the monosyllabic (from the Anglo-Saxon), each strand has two distinct functions: the polysyllabic words are often used when there is time for fanciful elaboration and rich description (which could be described as 'excessive rhetoric') while the monosyllabic occur when, literally, there is no other way of putting a basic question or comment - Juliet's "Do you love me? I know thou wilt say aye" is a classic example of both monosyllables and non-embellishment: with monosyllables, only the naked truth is being spoken, nothing is hidden

Monologues from Shakespeare's First Folio for Older Men: *The Comedies*

The Comedie of Errors
Merchant

In Syracusa was I borne, and wedde
1.1.36–61

Background: Duke Solinus, having explained why Egeon has been condemned to death, has ordered him to 'say in briefe the cause/ Why thou departedst from thy native home ? /And for what cause thou cam'st to Ephesus'. The following, hardly brief, explains exactly why: this speech sets up the initial circumstances, including marriage, becoming a father of identical twins, profitable and happy times:

Style: public address to one specific character in front of interested observers

Where: court, trial chamber, or even place of execution

To Whom: Solinus, Duke of Ephesus

# of Lines: 25

Probable Timing: 1.15 minutes

Take note: With the Duke's total change of heart from the death sentence to the attempted (though hand-tied) sympathetic help offered, it seems obvious that, whether consciously or no, the Merchant (Egeon) is a remarkably fine story teller: F's orthography clearly shows how.

Egeon

1   In Syracusa was I born, and wed
    Unto a woman, happy but for me,
    And by me, had not our hap been bad :
    With her I liv'd in joy ; our wealth increas'd
    By prosperous voyages I often made
    To [Epidamnium], till my factor's death,
    And the great care of goods at randon left,
    Drew me from kind embracements of my spouse;
    From whom my absence was not six months old
    Before herself (almost at fainting under
    The pleasing punishment that women bear)
    Had made provision for her following me,
    And soon, and safe, arrived where I was .

2   There had she not been long but she became
    A joyful mother of two goodly sons:
    And, which was strange, the one so like the other,
    As could not be distinguish'd but by names .

3   That very hour, and in the self -same inn,
    A [poor] mean woman was delivered
    Of such a burthen male, twins both alike .

4   Those, for their parents were exceeding poor,
    I bought, and brought up to attend my sons .

5   My wife, not meanly proud of two such boys,
    Made daily motions for our home return :
    Unwilling I agreed .

6   Alas, too soon
    We came aboard .

Egeon as Merchant

1   In Syracusa was I borne, and wedde
     Unto a woman, happy but for me,
     And by me ; had not our hap beene bad :
     With her I liv'd in joy, our wealth increast
     By prosperous voyages I often made
     To [Epidamium], till my factors death,
     And {the} great care of goods at randone left,
     Drew me from kinde embracements of my spouse;
     From whom my absence was not six moneths olde,
     Before her selfe (almost at fainting under
     The pleasing punishment that women beare)
     Had made provision for her following me,
     And soone, and safe, arrived where I was :
     There had she not beene long, but she became
     A joyfull mother of two goodly sonnes :
     And, which was strange, the one so like the other,
     As could not be distinguish'd but by names .

2   That very howre, and in the selfe-same Inne,
     A [ ] meane woman was delivered
     Of such a burthen Male, twins both alike :
     Those, for their parents were exceeding poore,
     I bought, and brought up to attend my sonnes .

3   My wife, not meanely prowd of two such boyes,
     Made daily motions for our home returne :
     Unwilling I agreed, alas, too soone wee came aboord .

- if the story itself were not enough, the single surround phrase

   " ; had not our hap beene bad : "

   is a clear indication as to Egeon's (the Merchant's) current state of mind and why the speech is so emotional throughout (4/27)

- and via sudden long spelling clusters, it seems that certain moments are burned into his brain (or, good raconteur as he is, he wants them burned into his audience's brain), such as 'my absence was not six moneths olde'; plus 'A joyfull mother of two goodly sonnes'; and 'That very howre, and in the selfe-same Inne/A meane woman was delivered'; together with 'My wife, not meanely prowd of two such boyes', and the doom-laden 'alas, too soone wee came aboord.'

- this latter point, the last line of this part of the speech, seems the most disturbing of all, for F sets it as an irregular (fourteen syllable) line: however, most modern texts reduce its significance by splitting it in two (a regular line of ten syllables followed by a short line of four), as the shading shows

- yet, in the sea of emotion, what is startling is that three key sets of story-telling details are presented totally unembellished

   "Unto a woman, happy but for me,/And by me ;"

   "With her I liv'd in joy, our wealth increast/By prosperous voyages I often made"

   "(almost at fainting under/The pleasing punishment that women beare)/Had made provision for her following me,"

   "And, which was strange, the one so like the other,/As could not be distinguish'd but by names ."

The Two Gentlemen of Verona
Duke

Why Phaeton (for thou art Merops sonne)
3.1.153–169

Background: just as Protheus planned, the Duke has uncovered Valentine's plan for eloping with Silvia, including the physical elements of both a letter and a rope ladder. The opening deals with Valentine over-extending himself by reaching for a Duke's daughter—the classical reference to Phaeton is to the young man who, through over-weening ambition and envy, attempted to drive Phoebus' (the sun-God's) chariot alone, and was destroyed by Jupiter once the horses proved unmanageable and threatened both heaven and earth with fiery destruction.

Style: a speech as a two-handed scene

Where: unspecified, somewhere in the Duke's palace

To Whom: Valentine

# of Lines: 17

Probable Timing: 0.55 minutes

Take Note: Though the sentence structures match, F's orthography reveals an interesting pattern of attempted self-control with occasional emotional flashes breaking through.

Duke

1 Why, Phaeton (for thou art Merop's son)
   Wilt thou aspire to guide the heavenly car,
   And with thy daring folly burn the world ?

2 Wilt thou reach stars, because they shine on thee ?

3 Go, base intruder, over weening slave,
   Bestow thy fawning smiles on equal mates,
   And think my patience (more [than] thy desert)
   Is privilege for thy departure hence .

4 Thank me for this, more [than] for all the favors
   Which (all too much) I have bestowed on thee .

5 But if thou linger in my territories
   Longer [than] swiftest expedition
   Will give thee time to leave our royal court,
   By heaven, my wrath shall far exceed the love
   I ever bore my daughter, or thyself .

6 Be gone, I will not hear thy vain excuse,
   But as thou lov'st thy life, make speed from hence .

Duke

1 Why Phaeton (for thou art Merops sonne)
   Wilt thou aspire to guide the heavenly Car ?
   And with thy daring folly burne the world ?

2 Wilt thou reach stars, because they shine on thee ?

3 Goe base Intruder, over-weening Slave,
   Bestow thy fawning smiles on equall mates,
   And thinke my patience, (more [then] thy desert)
   Is priviledge for thy departure hence .

4 Thanke me for this, more [then] for all the favors
   Which (all too-much) I have bestowed on thee .

5 But if thou linger in my Territories
   Longer [then] swiftest expedition
   Will give thee time to leave our royall Court,
   By heaven, my wrath shall farre exceed the love
   I ever bore my daughter, or thy selfe .

6 Be gone, I will not heare thy vaine excuse,
   But as thou lov'st thy life, make speed from hence .

- At first, the Duke seems to display self control, with the opening intellectually demeaning classical comparison (F #1, 3/1), followed by the acidly precise unembellished monosyllabic short sentence enquiry 'Wilt thou reach stars, because they shine on thee?';

- then passion begins to break through, with F #3's first line dismissal (2/1 in just the one line), leading to an emotional release from thereon in (2/9 in the remaining twelve lines).

- That the Duke is still attempting to maintain control can be seen in that from now on usually only one word per line shows any release: thus, the two small clusters in the middle of F #5, 'our royall Court' and the opening of F #6 'Be gone, I will not heare thy vaine excuse' are worth exploring for extra loss of control.

- That control is difficult to maintain can be seen in that after F #2 there are only three more unembellished lines, about the favors 'Which (all too-much) I have bestowed on thee.', and the need for Valentine to leave the Court as quickly as he can , with the warning not to linger 'Longer than swiftest expedition/Will give thee time to leave ... But as thou lovs't thy life, make speed from hence.'

The Taming of the Shrew

Baptista

Gentlemen, importune me no farther,
1.1.48–54, 92–104

Background: his first speech in the play, which sets up the difficulties facing the two local suitors for his youngest daughter Bianca—because, as all the locals know, the older, Kate, also known as Katherina, is such a scold that no man would willingly go near her.

Style: part of a three-handed scene, with others watching

Where: unspecified, but presumably a public place/street in Padua

To Whom: the old suitor Gremio, listed as a 'Pantelowne' (a Commed'ia type figure at his first entry), and the younger Hortentio, in front of both of his daughters Kate ('Katherina') and Bianca, with, unknown to all of them, the hidden Lucentio and Tranio watching what's going on

# of Lines: 17

Probable Timing: 0.55 minutes

Take Note: What is so startling about the speech is the totally unembellished seven line opening sentence (save for the proper name Katherina), suggesting that for some reason Baptista, is taking great efforts to remain calm (an attempt to avoid public embarrassment perhaps? or perhaps so as not to be overheard by Katherina?).

Baptista

1   Gentlemen, importune me no farther,
     For how I firmly am resolv'd you know :
     That is, not to bestow my youngest daughter
     Before I have a husband for the elder .

2   If either of you both love Katherina,
     Because I know you well, and love you well,
     Leave shall you have to court her at your pleasure .

3   And for I know {Bianca} taketh most delight
     In music, instruments, and poetry,
     Schoolmasters will I keep within my house,
     Fit to instruct her youth .

4   If you, Hortensio,
     Or, Signior Gremio, you, know any such,
     Prefer them hither ; for to cunning men
     I will be very kind, and liberal
     To mine own children in good bringing up,
     And so farewell .

5   Katherina, you may stay,
     For I have more to commune with Bianca .

Baptista

1   Gentlemen, importune me no farther,
    For how I firmly am resolv'd you know :
    That is, not to bestow my yongest daughter,
    Before I have a husband for the elder :
    If either of you both love Katherina,
    Because I know you well, and love you well,
    Leave shall you have to court her at your pleasure .

---

2   And for I know {Bianca} taketh most delight
    In Musicke, Instruments, and Poetry,
    Schoolemasters will I keepe within my house,
    Fit to instruct her youth .

3   If you Hortensio,
    Or signior Gremio you know any such,
    Preferre them hither : for to cunning men,
    I will be very kinde and liberall,
    To mine owne children, in good bringing up,
    And so farewell : Katherina you may stay,
    For I have more to commune with Bianca .

- This apparent need to stay calm is seen in the continuation of the speech, for the ever money-conscious Baptista seems to pulse back and forth between intellect, in the first two lines of F #2 (4/1) talking of Bianca's supposed joys in things artistic; and emotion, when talking about spending money on 'Schoolemasters' (the last two lines of F #2, 0/2).

- And this switching back and forth continues through F #3, where the direct appeal to Bianca's two rival suitors (2/0 in the first line and a half) turns again to emotion with reference to spending money ('kinde and liberall') on his own children (0/4 in the next three lines) and back to intellectual as he says farewell to all on stage, wishing to separate himself from his 'shrew' daughter, Katherina.

- Even the two intellectual passages in F #3 could be regarded as non-embellished (for all four capitalised words are proper names): if so, Baptista's struggle to maintain his sense of dignity becomes even more marked.

The Taming of the Shrew

Gremio

You may go to the divels dam
between 1.1.105–145

Background: Gremio's response to the prior speech of Baptista, and to Hortensio: this is his first major speech of the play.

Style: as part of a two handed scene

Where: unspecified, but presumably a public place/street in Padua

To Whom: to his younger Bianca-wooing rival, Hortensio

# of Lines: 8

Probable Timing: 0.30 minutes

Take Note: Again, a very careful speech, with the opening non-embellished short sentence suggesting the cursing out of Kate is not yelled but kept very quiet (in case she might hear and respond?).

Gremio

1   You may go to the devil's dam {.}

---

2 {†}   Think'st thou, Hortensio, though
     her father be very rich, any man is so very a fool to be
     married to hell ?

---

3   I cannot tell ;but I had as lief take her dowry
     with this condition : to be whipt at the high cross every
     morning .

---

4   I {will give } him the
     best horse in Padua to begin his wooing that would tho-
     roughly woo her, wed her, and bed her, and rid the
     house of her !

Gremio

1   You may go to the divels dam {.}

---

2 {†}   Think'st thou Hortensio, though
     her father be verie rich, any man is so verie a foole to be
     married to hell ?

---

3   I cannot tell : but I had as lief take her dowrie
     with this condition ; To be whipt at the hie crosse everie
     morning .

---

4   I {will give } him the
     best horse in Padua to begin his woing that would tho-
     roughly woe her, wed her, and bed her, and ridde the
     house of her .

- the three surround phrases comprising F #3 point to the depth of Gremio's loathing (and fear?) of Kate, especially with the only (emotional) semicolon of the speech

- interestingly, in F #3 the short spelling of what modern texts set as 'woo' is equated to that of grief, 'woe', suggesting it is almost choked back as something too distasteful to be spoken aloud—yet the other verb associated with Kate, the more desirable 'ridde', is given extra weight

- and there are a lot of other short spellings ('verie', 'dowrie', 'hie', everie', 'woing' as well as woe')—perhaps reinforcing the idea of distaste (or trying to prevent Kate from overhearing)

The Taming of the Shrew

Gremio

First, as you know, my house within the City
2.1.346–362

Background: at last Gremio makes his formal move in the wooing—dealing with Bianca's father as a matter of commerce, rather than dealing directly with her as a matter of love. Essentially Baptista has turned the whole thing into a bidding process for a commodity, having assured Gremio and the supposed Lucentio (Tranio in disguise) that whoever can offer the most in worldly goods shall have Bianca ('he…/that can assure my daughter greatest dower,/ Shall have my Biancas love.'). The following is Gremio's first offer (which turns out to be nowhere near enough, and whether Tranio's responses as Lucentio make Gremio aware of this is up to each production to decide).

Style: direct address to one person as part of a three handed scene

Where: in or about Baptista's home

To Whom: Baptista in front of Tranio disguised as Lucentio

# of Lines: 17

Probable Timing: 0.55 minutes

Gremio

1   First, as you know, my house within the city
     Is richly furnished with plate and gold,
     Basins and ewers to lave her dainty hands ;
     My hangings all of Tyrian tapestry ;
     In ivory coffers I have stuff'd my crowns ;
     In cypress chests my arras counterpoints,
     Costly apparel, tents, and canopies,
     Fine linen, Turkey cushions boss'd with pearl,
     [Valance] of Venice gold in needlework :
     Pewter and brass, and all things that belongs
     To house or housekeeping .

2   Then at my farm
     I have a hundred milch-kine to the [pail],
     Six score fat oxen standing in my stalls,
     And all things answerable to this portion .

3   Myself am strook in years, I must confess,
     And if I die tomorrow, this is hers,
     If whil'st I live she will be only mine .

Gremio

1   First, as you know, my house within the City
    Is richly furnished with plate and gold,
    Basons and ewers to lave her dainty hands :
    My hangings all of tirian tapestry :
    In Ivory cofers I have stuft my crownes :
    In Cypres chests my arras counterpoints,
    Costly apparell, tents, and Canopies,
    Fine Linnen, Turky cushions bost with pearle,
    [Vallens] of Venice gold, in needle worke :
    Pewter and brasse, and all things that belongs
    To house or house-keeping :then at my farme
    I have a hundred milch-kine to the [pail],
    Sixe-score fat Oxen standing in my stalls,
    And all things answerable to this portion .

2   My selfe am strooke in yeeres I must confesse,
    And if I die to morrow this is hers,
    If whil'st I live she will be onely mine .

- Gremio's opening salvo in the bidding war starts out very quietly (1/0 in the first four lines), with the initial listing of his worldly goods all unembellished

  "Is richly furnished with plate and gold,/Basons and ewers to lave her dainty hands : /My hangings all of tirian tapestry :"

  as if he were nervous and/or taking great care to get the words out

- with the last of the unembellished lines also being the first of the (only) two consecutive surround phrases in the speech 'My hangings all of tirian tapestry : /In Ivory cofers I have stuft my crownes : ', it would seem that Gremio is beginning to find his verbal feet

- for the next six and a half lines, dealing with all his city wealth (from 'In Ivory cofers' through to 'or house-keeping'), he becomes both in-tellectually and emotionally passionate (6/7)

- while the speech finishes almost totally emotionally (1/7 in the last three and a half lines of F #1 plus all of F #2)

- interestingly within this emotion, as the description of his ex-tra country wealth begins so he starts out in calm unembellished self-control once again ('I have a hundred milch-kine to the pale'), finishing the same way when hinting at even more matching wealth ('And all things answerable to this portion.')

- rather ingenuously (or nauseatingly, dependent upon your point of view), the final 'bribe' is also unembellished: 'And if I die to morrow this is hers' (the middle line of F #2)

The Taming of the Shrew

Gremio

A bridegroome say you ?
between 3.2.152–183

Background: since Tranio and Lucentio were busily planning strategy, neither witnessed the wedding ceremony for Kate and Petruchio, which, as Gremio tells the disguised Tranio in great detail, was hardly conventional.

Style: initially verse, and then, in the First Folio at least, prose, as part of a possible three-hander, though the real Lucentio might have left the stage as Gremio entered

Where: somewhere close to where the wedding took place, either the Church or Baptista's home

To Whom: the disguised Tranio, still believing him to be Lucentio, with perhaps the real Lucentio also present

# of Lines: 24

Probable Timing: 1.15 minutes

Take note: The shaded text shows where, as on several other occasions, F1 allows Gremio to slip from the polite formality of verse to somewhat more street smart and earthy prose as a key moment or overly-emotional mood gets the better of him. Most modern texts follow F2 and set the passage as verse, thus removing this potential character trait. They spoil the moment even further by taking F's onrushed F #4, which suggests Gremio just cannot stop the prose description from pouring out of him, and creating a much more rational recollection by splitting it into no fewer than seven sentences.

Gremio

1 A bridegroom, say you ? '

2 Why, he's a devil, a devil, a very fiend .

3 I'll tell you, Sir Lucentio : when the priest
Should ask if Katherine should be his wife,
"Ay, by gogs wouns," quoth he, and swore so loud,
That all amaz'd the Priest let fall the book,
And as he stoop'd again to take it up,
This mad-brain'd bridegroom took him such a cuff
That down fell Priest and book, and book and priest.

4 "Now take them up," quoth he, "if any list" .

5 {The wench} trembled and shook ;for why, he stamp'd
and swore
As if the vicar meant to cozen him .

6 But after many ceremonies done,
He calls for wine .

7   "A health !" quoth he, as if
He had been aboard, carousing to his mates
After a storm, quaff'd off the muscadel,
And threw the sops all in the sexton's face :
Having no other reason
But that his beard grew thin and hungerly,
And seem'd to ask him sops as he was drinking .

8 This done, he took the Bride about the neck,
And kiss'd her lips with such a clamorous smack
That at the parting all the church did echo .

9 And I seeing this, came thence for very shame,
And after me I know the rout is coming.

10 Such a mad marriage never was before .

11 Hark, hark, I hear the minstrels play .

Gremio

1   A bridegroome say you ? '

---

2   Why hee's a devill, a devill, a very fiend .

---

3   Ile tell you sir Lucentio ; when the Priest
     Should aske if Katherine should be his wife,
     I, by goggs woones quoth he, and swore so loud,
     That all amaz'd the Priest let fall the booke,
     And as he stoop'd againe to take it up,
     This mad-brain'd bridegroome tooke him such a cuffe,
     That downe fell Priest and booke, and booke and Priest,
     Now take them up quoth he, if any list .

---

4   {The wench} trembled and shooke : for why, he stamp'd and
     swore, as if the Vicar meant to cozen him :but after ma-
     ny ceremonies done, hee calls for wine, a health quoth
     he, as if he had beene aboord, carowsing to his Mates af-
     ter a storme, quaft off the Muscadell, and threw the sops
     all in the Sextons face :having no other reason, but that
     his beard grew thinne and hungerly, and seem'd to aske
     him sops as hee was drinking :This done, hee tooke the
     Bride about the necke, and kist her lips with such a cla-
     morous smacke, that at the parting all the Church did
     eccho :and I seeing this, came thence for very shame, and
     after mee I know the rout is comming, such a mad mar-
     ryage never was before : harke, harke, I heare the min-
     strels play .

- the opening two short sentences, in themselves an indication of the uncommon moment about to be described, start emotionally (0/4)

- that the story affects Gremio emotionally (whether amazement or amusement is up to each reader to decide) can be seen in the surround phrase that opens F #3 ('Ile tell you, sir Lucentio ; ') ending as it does with the only emotional semicolon in the speech

- and, after F #3's intellectual two line opening (3/1), the recollection becomes highly emotional (3/9 in the remaining six lines of F #3; 7/21 in the thirteen and a half prose lines of F #4)

- thus, within the emotional sea, the occasional cluster release shows Gremio illustrating or commenting upon certain moments burned into his brain such as: 'hee's a devill, a devill'; by 'goggs woones' (i.e. 'God's wounds'); 'This mad-brain'd bridegroome tooke him such a cuffe, / That downe fell Priest and booke, and booke and Priest,'; 'as if he had beene aboord, carowsing to his Mates after a storme'; 'hee tooke the Bride about the necke,'

- the art of story-telling doesn't seem to escape him either, for the end of F #3 finishes with an incredibly calm 'Now take them up, quoth he, if any list', and if not the art of story-telling, then this particular incident (Petruchio's knocking the Priest and bible to the floor) seems to have struck Gremio almost dumb

Loves Labour's Lost
Don Armado/Braggart

I doe affect the very ground (which is base)
1.2.167–185

Background: Don Armado (the Braggart) is kept at the court for his entertainment value—described by Ferdinand as 'A man in all the worlds new fashion planted/that hath a mint of phrases in his braine:/One, who the musicke of his owne vaine tongue,/ Doth ravish like enchanting harmonie', for, as a Spaniard, he mangles or overelaborates or creates malapropisms in nearly every speech. He too is supposed to abstain from contact with women. Unfortunately, he has fallen for Jaquenetta, doubly unfortunate in that, however impoverished, he is supposedly of noble birth and she a simple country girl who cannot read. The following is his first solo address to the audience just after she has exited with her true beau, Costard the Clowne.

Style: solo

Where: unspecified, within the palace grounds

To Whom: direct audience address

# of Lines: 18

Probable Timing: 0.55 minutes

Take Note: F's orthography reveals clearly defined stages of an older man finding a way to break his oath so as to woo a young woman.

Don Armado

1   I do affect the very ground (which is base)
where her shoe (which is baser) guided by her foot
(which is basest) doth tread .

2   I shall be forsworn (which
is a great argument of falsehood) if I love .

3   And how can
that be true love, which is falsely attempted ?

4   Love is a familiar ; Love is a devil ; there is no evil angel but
Love.

5   Yet [was Sampson] so tempted, and he had an excellent strength ; yet was Salomon so seduced, and he had
a very good wit .

6   Cupid's butt-shaft is too hard for Hercules' club, and therefore too much odds for a Spaniard's rapier .

7   The first and second cause will not serve
my turn ; the passado he respects not, the duello he
regards not : his disgrace is to be called boy, but his
glory is to subdue men .

8   Adieu, valor, rust, rapier, be
still, drum, for your manager is in love ; yea, he loveth .

9   Assist me, some extemporal god of rhyme, for I am sure I
shall turn sonnet .

10   Devise, wit, write, pen, for I am for
whole volumes in folio .

Braggart

1   I doe affect the very ground (which is base)
where her shooe (which is baser) guided by her foote
(which is basest) doth tread .

2   I shall be forsworn (which
is a great argument of falshood) if I love .

3   And how can
that be true love, which is falsly attempted ?

4   Love is a familiar, Love is a Divell .

5   There is no evill Angell but
Love, yet [Sampson was] so tempted, and he had an excellent strength : Yet was Salomon so seduced, and hee had
a very good witte .

6   Cupids Butshaft is too hard for Hercules Clubbe, and therefore too much ods for a Spa-
niards Rapier : The first and second cause will not serve
my turne : the Passado hee respects not, the Duello he
regards not ; his disgrace is to be called Boy, but his
glorie is to subdue men .

7   Adue Valour, rust Rapier, bee
still Drum, for your manager is in love ; yea hee loveth .

8   Assist me some extemporall god of Rime, for I am sure I
shall turne Sonnet .

9   Devise Wit, write Pen, for I am for
whole volumes in folio .

- the speech starts very carefully, only slightly emotional as Armado confesses his total adoration of Jaquenetta (0/2, F #1), and then completely unembellished as he uncovers the double dilemma of being dishonourable and how that might affect 'true love' (F #2-3): thus it's interesting to note the words 'falshood' and 'falsly' are both set in their withheld (short-spelling) form

- and then, as with Berowne earlier (speech #3 above), as he determines to define 'Love', so the releases start coming thick and fast

- with the the first definitions, 'Love' as a 'Divell' and references to how men of strength (Sampson) and intelligence (Solomon) were felled by it, so Armado becomes highly passionate (7/5 in just the three and a half lines of F #4-5)

- the wonderful realisation/excuse that if even Hercules cannot withstand 'Love' how can he, becomes an exercise in mental self deception (9/3 in the six lines of F #6): and this passage is well served by F's onrush allowing the thoughts to flow: most modern texts spoil this by splitting the sentence in two, with mt. #6 offering the chop-logic excuse that if Hercules cannot withstand love how can he, and mt. #7 dealing with how each of his military defences will be useless in protecting him from 'Love'

- in his moment of self-redefinition, with the farewell to arms, the admittance of being 'in love' and the appeal for help from a new source (the 'god of Rime'), Armado becomes passionate (5/5, F #7-8)—though 'Adue' and 'Rime' are short spelled

- and in the final self-encouragement to become a poet, Armado becomes intellectual once more (2/0, F #9)

Loves Labour's Lost

Braggart

Sir, it is the Kings most sweet pleasure and affection
between 5.1.87–116

Background: with the failure of the Russian Masque, the four young
men have charged Armado to prepare an entertainment for the
French visitors. He, in turn, has come to ask the locals, especially
the schoolmaster/pedant Holofernes for help: hence the following-

Style: as part of four handed scene

Where: unspecified, but presumably either near Holofernes' home/
school, or close to where he and Nathaniel have just dined 'at the
fathers of a certaine Pupill of mine'

To Whom: Holofernes, the curate Sir Nathaniel, and Constable Dull

# of Lines: 20

Probable Timing: 1.00 minutes

Take Note: The language conveys Armado's palpable excitement, so,
not surprisingly, the speech is much more emotional than intellectual (13/23 overall).

Don Armado

1   Sir, it is the King's most sweet pleasure and affection, to congratulate the Princess at her pavilion in
the posteriors of this day, which the rude multitude call
the afternoon.

---

2 {†} The King is a noble gentleman, and my familiar, I do assure ye, very good friend {.}

---

3   For I
must tell thee it will please his Grace (by the world)
sometime to lean upon my poor shoulder, and with
his royal finger, thus, dally with my excrement, with my
mustachio ; but sweet heart, let that pass .

4   By the world,
I recount no fable : some certain special honors it
pleaseth his greatness to impart to Armado, a soldier,
a man of travel, that hath seen the world ; but let that
pass .

5   The very all of all is—but, sweet heart, I do implore
secrecy- that the King would have me present the
Princess (sweet chuck) with some delightful ostenta-
tion, or show, or pageant, or antic, or fire-work .

6   Now, understanding that the curate and your sweet self
are good at such eruptions, and sudden breaking out of
mirth (as it were), I have acquainted you withal, to
the end to crave your assistance .

Braggart

1　Sir, it is the Kings most sweet pleasure and affection, to congratulate the Princesse at her Pavilion, in
the posteriors of this day, which the rude multitude call
the afternoone .

---

2 {†} The King is a noble Gentleman, and my familiar, I doe assure ye very good friend {.}

3　　　　　　　　　　　　　　　　　　For I
must tell thee it will please his Grace (by the world)
sometime to leane upon my poore shoulder, and with
his royall finger thus dallie with my excrement, with my
mustachio : but sweet heart let that passe .

4　　　　　　　　　　　　　　　　By the world
I recount no fable, some certaine speciall honours it
pleaseth his greatnesse to impart to Armado a Souldier,
a man of travell, that hath seene the world : but let that
passe ; the very all of all is :but sweet heart, I do implore
secrecie, that the King would have mee present the
Princesse (sweet chucke) with some delightfull ostenta-
tion, or show, or pageant, or anticke, or fire-worke :
Now, understanding that the Curate and your sweet self
are good at such eruptions, and sodaine breaking out of
myrth (as it were) I have acquainted you withall, to
the end to crave your assistance .

- the one moment of capitalised release ('the Princesse at her Pavilion') seems to allow the actor alliterative fun with Armado's love of language and florid self-expression

- and at times it seems that even he is aware that his mouth is running away with him, for the surround phrases show him reigning in his enthusiasm ' : but sweet heart, let that passe . ' followed by ' : but let that passe ; the very all of all is : '

- yet at least he starts out with some semblance of controlled passion (5/3, F #1-2) as he lays in the preamble as to why he has approached the two supposed learned men known to be good at 'eruptions'

- but, as the conversation veers off topic as to how he, Armado, is regarded (or would like to be regarded) by royalty, he becomes highly emotional (6/17, F #3 and F #4's first eight lines—to the final colon)

- thus the few clusters of emotional release point to where his revery (of his—supposed?—relations with the King) seems to be getting the better of him: 'sometime to leane upon my poore shoulder'; 'some certaine speciall honours'; 'a Souldier, a man of travell that hath seene the world'

- however, finally getting back to the point at hand and asking for their assistance, Armado brings himself back to a modicum of self-control (2/3, the last four lines of the speech)

A Midsommer Nights Dreame

Bottome

{†} A Lover that kills himselfe most gallantly for love ?
1.2.24–41

Background: the producer of the play 'Pyramus and Thisbie', Quince, is a carpenter, and whether he is used to theatrics, and whether he wrote the play himself, is up to each production to decide. In the following, Bottome (the most theatrically experienced of the group) provides his initial response to both Quince and his fellow actors about being offered the lead, a romantic rather than a swash-buckling role. One note: the first line, marked {†} is taken from Quince's earlier explanation of the role.

Style: group address as part of a six-handed scene

Where: unspecified, but somewhere in Athens

To Whom: Quince, Flute, Starveling, Snug, and Snout

# of Lines: 11

Probable Timing: 0.40 minutes

Take Note: F's orthography suggests Bottome's love of the theatre knows no bounds.

Bottom

1 {†} A lover, that kills himself most [gallant] for love {?}

2   That will ask some tears in the true perfor-
     ming of it .

3   If I do it, let the audience look to their eyes.

4   I will move storms; I will condole in some measure .

5   To the rest—yet my chief humor is for a tyrant .

6   I could
     play Ercles rarely, or a part to tear a cat in, to make all
     split.

7   "The raging rocks
          And shivering shocks
          Shall break the locks
             Of prison gates;
          And phibbus' car
       Shall shinevfrom far ,
          And make and mar
          The foolish Fates ."

8   This was lofty !

9   Now name the rest of the players .

10   This
     is Ercles' vein, a tyrant's vein ; a lover is more condo-
     ling .

Bottome

1 {†} A Lover that kills himselfe most [gallantly] for love {?}

2   That will aske some teares in the true perfor-
     ming of it : if I do it, let the audience looke to their eies :
     I will moove stormes ; I will condole in some measure .

3   To the rest yet, my chiefe humour is for a tyrant .

4   I could
     play Ercles rarely, or a part to teare a Cat in, to make all
     split the raging Rocks ; and shivering shocks shall break
     the locks of prison gates, and Phibbus carre shall shine
     from farre, and make and marre the foolish Fates .

5   This
     was lofty .

6   Now name the rest of the Players .

7   This
     is Ercles vaine, a tyrants vaine : a lover is more condo-
     ling .

- the surround phrases underscore Bottome's passionate belief as to how theatre should work from a performer's viewpoint, as the whole of F #2 and F #7 clearly show

- the short sentences (F #1, #3, #5, and #6) also focus totally on the theatre, the first three on himself, the latter on more practical matters

- after a careful musing of what he is asked to play (F #1, 1/0), emotions begin to flow as he envisages perfomance ideas (0/7, F #2-3)

- in performing before them (F #4), he starts out intellectually (2/1 in the first two lines) but finishes, as many an experienced amateur performer will, somewhat more emotionally (2/3 in the last line and a half)

- within the midst of F #4's 'performance' comes a most wickedly wonderful 'performer's moment' of deliberate quiet, viz. 'and shivering shockes shall break the locks of prison gates'

- one note about F #4: F/Qq all present Bottome's 'raging rocks' extravaganza (shaded) passage as prose, most modern texts lay it out according to its rhyming pattern: one reading of the source text could be that Bottome is not completely comfortable with (perhaps is even inventing) the doggerel, certainly it is not presented as accomplished and polished speech—even though the modern restructuring presents the material as 'pure' verse which it presumes Bottome can handle with ease

- then, post performance, comes a moment of relative 'calm' (1/0, F #6-7), though whether real or theatrical is up to each actor to explore, with the summary being emotional once more (1/2, F #7)

A Midsommer Nights Dreame

Bottome

Masters, you ought to consider with your selves, to
between 3.1.29–46

Background: following the casting meeting and now assembling in the woods to rehearse so that they are not 'dog'd with company' nor their 'devices known', Bottome and the others have had time to inspect the script, and have come up with a problem.

Style: group address as part of a six-handed scene

Where: somewhere in the woods near the Fairies' haunts

To Whom: Quince, Flute, Starveling, Snug, & Snout

# of Lines: 14

Probable Timing: 0.45 minutes

Take Note: Once more, Bottome's mind and emotions come into play as the company still tries to come to terms with how to avoid getting into trouble with the Duke when presenting the 'Lyon'...

Bottom

1   Masters, you ought to consider with yourselves, to
bring in (God shield us !) a lion among ladies, is a most
dreadful thing ; for there is not a more fearful wild-
fowl [than] your lion living ; and we ought to look
[to't] .

---

2 {†} {Y}ou must name his name, and half his face
must be seen though the lion's neck, and he himself
must speak through, saying thus, or to the same defect :
"Ladies", or " Fair Ladies, I would wish you", or "I would
request you", or "I would entreat you, not to fear, not to
tremble : my life for yours .

3   If you think I come hither
as a lion, it were pity of my life .

4   No ! I am no such
thing ; I am a man as other men are" ; and there indeed let
him name his name, and tell [them] plainly he is Snug the
joiner .

Bottome

1   Masters, you ought to consider with your selves, to
     bring in (God shield us) a Lyon among Ladies, is a most
     dreadfull thing .

2   For there is not a more fearefull wilde
     foule [then] your Lyon living : and wee ought to looke
     [to it] .

---

3 {†} {Y}ou must name his name, and halfe his face
     must be seene though the Lyons necke, and he himselfe
     must speake through, saying thus, or to the same defect ;
     Ladies, or faire Ladies, I would wish you, or I would
     request you, or I would entreat you, not to feare, not to
     tremble : my life for yours .

4   If you thinke I come hither
     as a Lyon, it were pitty of my life .

5   No, I am no such
     thing, I am a man as other men are ; and there indeed let
     him name his name, and tell [him] plainly hee is Snug the
     joyner .

- ... at least at the beginning (3/2, F #1)

- but then, as the problem is fully spelled out (F #2) and an answer begins to present itself (the first three lines of F #3), so his emotions have full sway (2/12 in just five lines)

- and though his intellect comes to the fore for a moment as the performer's imagination takes over once more (2/1, the last two and a half lines of F #3), his emotions are soon in full cry as he nears the conclusion of the performance he envisages for the performer of the Lyon (1/3, F #4)

- once again, the performers 'quiet moment' strikes as he suggests that the Lyon finishes with an unembellished surround phrase '. No, I am no such thing, I am a man as other men are ; '—without the extra heavy punctuation (an exclamation mark and two semicolons) offered by most modern texts

A Midsommer Nights Dreame

Bottom/Clowne

When my cue comes, call me, and I will answer .
4.1.200–219

Background: though the spell on him has been removed and he is back to his human play-rehearsal self, Bottome still has some memories of what happened when he was an 'Asse'—though it appears he's not going to voice them.

Style: solo

Where: somewhere in the woods

To Whom: direct audience address

# of Lines: 18

Probable Timing: 0.55 minutes

Take Note: The highly unusual proliferation of very short sentences is a sure sign that Bottome is unable to deflect what he has undergone with his usual long and complex thoughts.

Bottom

1   When my cue comes, call me, and I will answer .

2   My next is, "Most faire Pyramus."

3   Hey ho !

4   Peter Quince !
     Flute the bellows-mender !

5   Snout the tinker !

6   Starve-
     ling !

7   Gods my life, stol'n hence, and left me asleep !

9   I
     have had a most rare vision .

10   I [have] had a dream, past the wit
     of man, to say, what dream it was .

11   Man is but an ass,
     if he go about ['t]expound this dream .

12   Methought I
     was—there is no man can tell what .

13   Methought I was,
     and methought I had—but man is but a patch'd fool,
     if he will offer to say what methought I had .

14   The eye of
     man hath not heard, the ear of man hath not seen, man's
     hand is not able to taste, his tongue to conceive, nor his
     heart to report, what my dream was .

15   I will get Peter
     Quince to write a ballad of this dream.

16   It shall be called
     "Bottom's Dream", because it hath no bottom ; and I will
     sing it in the latter end of a play, before the Duke .

17   Per-
     adventure, to make it the more gracious, I shall sing it
     at her death .

Clowne

1   When my cue comes, call me, and I will answer .

2   My next is, most faire Piramus .

3   Hey ho Peter Quince ?
Flute the bellowes-mender ?

4   Snout the tinker ?

5   Starveling ?

6   Gods my life !

7   Stolne hence, and left me asleepe : I
have had a most rare vision .

8   I [ ] had a dreame, past the wit
of man, to say, what dreame it was .

9   Man is but an Asse,
if he goe about [to expound] this dreame .

10   Me-thought I
was, there is no man can tell what .

11   Me-thought I was,
and me-thought I had .

12   But man is but a patch'd foole,
if he will offer to say, what me-thought I had .

13   The eye of
man hath not heard, the eare of man hath not seen, mans
hand is not able to taste, his tongue to conceive, nor his
heart to report, what my dreame was .

14   I will get Peter
Quince to write a ballet of this dreame, it shall be called
Bottomes Dreame, because it hath no bottome ; and I will
sing it in the latter end of a play, before the Duke .

15   Peradventure, to make it the more gracious, I shall sing it
at her death .

- in addition, the very small scale releases scattered throughout the speech suggest that Bottome is still lost in his world of (Fairy) wonders

- the factual/intellectual releases are almost completely restricted to the 'real' world of his friends (F #2-6, 7/2); while the mix of intellectual and emotional passion focuses on the forthcoming performance (5/4, F #14)…

- …the recollection of his 'rare vision' is almost completely emotional (1/9, F #7-13)

- after the quiet awaking (F #1), the majority of the other unembellished lines relate to what he has just experienced

    "I have had a most rare vision."

  and, with the exception of the one word 'foole'

    "Me-thought I was, there is no man can tell what . Me-thought I was, and me-thought I had . But man is but a patch'd foole, if he will offer to say, what me-thought I had ."

- however, with the exception of the word Duke, the last line of F #14 and all of F's final #15, which put forward the possibility of his singing in the forthcoming play are also unembellished (the dream of possible success almost taking his breath away perhaps?)

- the surround phrases underscore the most important moment within each of the three worlds, first his being abandoned by his friends coupled with a syntactically incorrect linking to what happened thereafter 'Stolne hence and left me asleepe : I have had a most rare vision . ', and then the hopes of theatrical success (perhaps leading to his becoming one of the Duke's favoured actors) ' ; and I will sing it in the latter end of a play, before the Duke . '

A Midsommer Nights Dreame

Theseus

More strange then true .

5.1.2–22

Background: their marriage having taken place, at last, Theseus and Hippolita are waiting for the two other just-married couples (Helena and Demetrius, Hermia and Lysander) and the provider of the evening's entertainment to join them. They are discussing the story told to them by the other two couples of their night's adventures.

Style: speech as part of a two handed scene

Where: somewhere in the palace where a post-supper pre-wedding bed entertainment is to be offered

To Whom: his new bride Hippolita

# of Lines: 20

Probable Timing: 1.00 minutes

Take Note: While Theseus still shows some swaths of self-control, the speech is nowhere near as logical as elsewhere in the play. The shaded text points to just how much F suggests that here Theseus is lost in his own imagination and is attempting to reach an understanding The modern texts' poetical restructuring smoothes away both awkwardness and excitement, creating somewhat bland posturing where half-formed new concepts originally existed.

Theseus

1   More strange [than] true .

2   I never may believe

3   These antic fables, nor these fairy toys.

4   Lovers and madmen have such seething brains,
Such shaping fantasies, that apprehend
More [than] cool reason ever comprehends .

5   The lunatic, the lover, and the poet
Are of imagination all compact .

6   One sees more devils [than] vast hell can hold ;
That is the madman .

7   The lover, all as frantic,
Sees Helen's beauty in a brow of Egypt .

8   The poet's eye, in a fine frenzy rolling,
Doth glance from heaven to earth, from earth to heaven ;
And as imagination bodies forth
The forms of things unknown, the poet's pen
Turns them to shapes, and gives to aery nothing
A local habitation, and a name .

9   Such tricks hath strong imagination,
That if it would but apprehend some joy,
It comprehends some bringer of that joy .

10   Or in the night, imagining some fear,
How easy is a bush suppos'd a bear !

Theseus

1   More strange [then] true .

2   I never may beleeve
These anticke fables, nor these Fairy toyes,
Lovers and mad men have such seething braines,
Such shaping phantasies, that apprehend more
[Then] coole reason ever comprehends .

3   The Lunaticke, the Lover, and the Poet,
Are of imagination all compact .

4   One sees more divels [then] vaste hell can hold ;
That is the mad man .

5   The Lover, all as franticke,
Sees Helens beauty in a brow of Egipt .

6   The Poets eye in a fine frenzy rolling, doth glance
From heaven to earth, from earth to heaven .

7   And as imagination bodies forth the forms of things
Unknowne ; the Poets pen turnes them to shapes,
And gives to aire nothing, a locall habitation,
And a name .

8   Such tricks hath strong imagination,
That if it would but apprehend some joy,
It comprehends some bringer of that joy .

9   Or in the night, imagining some feare,
How easie is a bush suppos'd a Beare ?

- the philosophical assessment seems to force Theseus to a very quiet and controlled exploration, as all the non-embellished phrases seem to suggest, starting with the short sentence

  "More strange [then] true."

moving into

  "Such shaping phantasies"
  "From heaven to earth, from earth to heaven./And as imagination bodies forth the forms of things"

realising that

  "Such tricks hath strong imagination,/That if it would but apprehend some joy,/It comprehends some bringer of that joy."

- as he expresses his skepticism, the speech opens emotionally (1/5, F #1-2) and closes equally emotionally as he tries to justify the skepticism (2/6, F #7-8),

- and, while the central section contains the intellectual exploration (7/3, F #3-6), he may not be as controlled as most modern texts would indicate, for, as footnote #4 explains, his struggle to understand comes at the cost of a very irregular line structure in F #6, and extends into the emotional F #7, suggesting that the exploration is more than somewhat taxing

- which is confirmed by the two emotional semicolons in F #4 and F #7

The Merchant of Venice
Shylocke

Anthonio is a good man . My meaning in saying he is a
between 1.3.12–39

Background: this is Shylocke's first major speech in his opening sequence in the play, as Bassanio is negotiating for his much needed
loan.

Style: as part of a two-handed scene

Where: unspecified, in some public space—possibly the Rialto

To Whom: Bassanio

# of Lines: 20

Probable Timing: 1.00 minutes

Take Note: Prior to this speech, the opening twelve lines of F (and the
quarto) could be read as either verse or prose (though most modern
texts set the passage as prose). Bassanio has questioned Shylocke's
possible maligning of Anthonio's reputation—and if the scene
opened in verse, by this point whatever forced verse of polite ele-
gance the scene might have started with would disappear.

Shylock

1   Antonio is a good man .

2   My meaning in saying he is a
good man, is to have you understand me that he is sufficient .

3   Yet his means are in supposition : he hath an argo-
sy bound to Tripolis, another to the Indies; I understand moreover upon the [Ryalto], he hath a third at Mexi-
co, a fourth for England, and other ventures he hath
squand'red abroad .

4   But ships are but boards, sailors but
men ; there be land rats and water rats, water thieves
and land thieves, I mean pirates, and then there is the
peril of waters, winds, and rocks .

5   The man is notwithstanding sufficient .

6   Three thousand ducats : I think I may
take his bond .

7   {A}nd that I may be assured, I will bethinkme .

8   May I speak with Antonio ?

9   {I will not} smell pork, {I will not} eat of the habitation
which your prophet the Nazarite conjur'd the devil
into .

10   I will buy with you, sell with you, talk with
you, walk with you, and so following ; but I will
not eat with you, drink with you, nor pray with you .

11   What news on the [Ryalto] ?

12   Who is he comes here ?

Shylocke

1   Anthonio is a good man .

2   My meaning in saying he is a
     good man, is to have you understand me that he is suffi{ci}-
     ent, yet his meanes are in supposition : he hath an Argo-
     sie bound to Tripolis, another to the Indies, I under-
     stand moreover upon the [Ryalta], he hath a third at Mexi-
     co, a fourth for England, and other ventures hee hath
     squandred abroad, but ships are but boords, Saylers but
     men, there be land rats, and water rats, water theeves
     and land theeves, I meane Pyrats, and then there is the
     perrill of waters, windes, and rocks : the man is notwith-
     standing sufficient, three thousand ducats, I thinke I may
     take his bond .

3   {A}nd that I may be assured, I will bethinke mee,
     may I speake with Anthonio ?

4   {I will not} smell porke, {I will not} eate of the habitation
     which your Prophet the Nazarite conjured the divell
     into : I will buy with you, sell with you, talke with
     you, walke with you, and so following : but I will
     not eate with you, drinke with you, nor pray with you .

5   What newes on the [Ryalta], who is he comes here ?

- F's long sentence #2 allows Shylocke to easily, almost casually, assess and dismiss Anthonio's financial situation: by splitting the sentence into five, most modern texts make it a much more determined and calculated exploration

- that he knows Anthonio has very deep financial pockets might lie in the three unembellished phrases

  "Anthonio is a good man ."
  "My meaning in saying he is a good man, is to have you understand me that he is sufficient,"
  "the man is notwithstanding sufficient, three thousand ducats,"

  which in turn suggests the rest is flim-flam to earn more loan points

- the majority of both spelling and capitals lies mainly in two places:

- the first comes in two contrasting sweeps in F #2, where in listing Anthonio's assets Shylocke's careful intellectual analyzing capitals come to the fore (F #2's first six lines, 6/2), to be immediately followed by a much more emotional statement of the risks involved (2/7, the rmainder of F #2) plus F #3's request to speak to Anthonio (1/3)

- traditionally actors have made two words of Ff's 'Pyrats', pronouncing it as 'Py-rats' so as to pun on the earlier images of the 'land' and 'water' rats: one commentator furthers this by offering 'pier rats' for the original word

- and emotions continue in F #4 as he refuses to break bread with the Christians (2/7), emphasised by the firmness of the long surround lines that finish the sentence, ' : I will buy with you, sell with you, talke with you, walke with you, and so following : but I will not eate with you, drinke with you, nor pray with you . ', themselves heightened by being monosyllabic save the one word 'following'

The Merchant of Venice
Shylock/Jew

How like a fawning publican he lookes .
1.3.41–52

Background: Anthonio has now joined the loan-seeking Bassanio
and Shylocke. While he and Bassanio talk, Shylocke reveals his in-
nermost feelings about Anthonio, with whom Shylocke is locked in
a mutually loathing relationship.

Style: aside

Where: unspecified, in some public space—possibly the Rialto

To Whom: direct audience address

# of Lines: 12

Probable Timing: 0.40 minutes

Take Note: The underlying orthography of the F text beautifully ex-
pands the statement of hatred clearly visible in the modern texts.

Shylock

1   How like a fawning publican he looks !

2   I hate him for he is a Christian ;
But more, for that in low simplicity
He lends out money gratis, and brings down
The rate of usance here with us in Venice .

3   If I can catch him once upon the hip,
I will feed fat the ancient grudge I bear him .

4   He hates our sacred nation, and he rails
Even there where merchants most do congregate
On me, my bargains, and my [well-won]thrift,
Which he calls interest .

5   Cursed be my tribe
If I forgive him .

Jew

1   How like a fawning publican he lookes .

2   I hate him for he is a Christian :
But more, for that in low simplicitie
He lends out money gratis, and brings downe
The rate of usance here with us in Venice .

3   If I can catch him once upon the hip,
I will feede fat the ancient grudge I beare him .

4   He hates our sacred Nation, and he railes
Even there where Merchants most doe congregate
On me, my bargaines, and my [well-worne] thrift,
Which he cals interrest : Cursed be my Trybe
If I forgive him .

- F clearly shows that, while Shylocke is in relative control of himself at the start of the speech (just six embellishments in seven lines in the opening three sentences, 2/4), as the second part of the speech starts at F #4, there is a sudden explosive release of ten embellishments (4/6) in just four and a half lines as Shylocke narrows in on Anthonio's presumed hatred of things Hebraic

- it's fascinating where the emotional (long-spelled) words are found, for nearly all of them are spoken at the end of a phrase or line, as if the words were being forced out of his mouth: the same can also be found for the first two of six capitals

- the two surround phrases

  " . I hate him for he is a Christian : " and " : Cursed be my Trybe/
     If I forgive him ."

  make Shylocke's focus and future actions absolutely unequivocally clear

- the fact that this last phrase ends the speech as somewhat of a blurt ending in F #4 adds great power to the curse: however, the inevitability of this powerful statement is rather gutted when set as a deliberate (even rational) new sentence by most modern

The Merchant of Venice
Shylocke

Signior Anthonio, many a time and oft
1.3.106–129

Background: the following is triggered by Anthonio's asking 'Well Shylocke, shall we be beholding to you/', a seemingly innocent question. However, immediately prior to the question Anthonio has revealed his true feelings about Shylocke 'The divell can cite scripture for his purpose,/An evill soule...', (speech #2 above) in a remark meant either as an aside or deliberately for Shylocke to overhear.

Style: part of a three-handed scene

Where: unspecified, in some public space—possibly the Rialto

To Whom: Anthonio

# of Lines: 23

Probable Timing: 1.10 minutes

Take Note: While critics suggest the Elizabethan Shylocke was meant to be regarded both as a figure of fun and a villain, there is a modern (and a naturally humanist) political correctness tendency to recast Shylocke as a dignified and sympathetic victim. The modern sentence restructuring of this speech often contributes to this revision, for whereas the modern explanation seems quite reasonable, the seething ripples underneath the F text is a constant reminder of Shylocke's disturbed anger and loathing.

Shylock

1   Signior Antonio, many a time and oft
     In the Rialto you have rated me
     About my moneys and my usances .

2   Still have I born it with a patient shrug
     (For suff'rance is the badge of all our tribe) .

3   You call me misbeliever, cut-throat dog,
     And [spit] upon my Jewish gaberdine,
     And all for use of that which is mine own .

4   Well then, it now appears you need my help .

5   Go to then, you come to me, and you say,
     "Shylock, we would have moneys", you say so -
     You, that did void your rheum upon my beard,
     And foot me as you spurn a stranger cur
     Over your threshold; moneys is your suit .

6   What should I say to you ?

7   Should I not say,
     "Hath a dog money ?

8   Is it possible
     A cur [can] lend three thousand ducats? "

9   Or
     Shall I bend low, and in a bondman's key,
     With bated breath, and whisp'ring humbleness,
     Say this :
     "Fair sir, you [spat] on me on Wednesday last,
     You spurn'd me such a day, another time
     You call'd me dog ; and for these courtesies
     I'll lend you thus much moneys ."

Shylocke

1   Signior Anthonio, many a time and oft
     In the Ryalto you have rated me
     About my monies and my usances :
     Still have I borne it with a patient shrug,
     (For suffrance is the badge of all our Tribe .)

2   You call me misbeleever, cut-throate, dog,
     And [spet] upon my Jewish gaberdine,
     And all for use of that which is mine owne .

3   Well then, it now appeares you neede my helpe :
     Goe to then, you come to me, and you say,
     Shylocke, we would have moneyes, you say so :
     You that did voide your rume upon my beard,
     And foote me as you spurne a stranger curre
     Over your threshold, moneyes is your suite .

4   What should I say to you ?
                              Should I not say,

5   Hath a dog money ?

6   Is it possible
     A curre should lend three thousand ducats ? or
     Shall I bend low, and in a bond-mans key
     With bated breath, and whispring humblenesse,
     Say this : Faire sir, you [spet]on me on Wednesday last ;
     You spurn'd me such a day ; another time
     You cald me dog : and for these curtesies
     Ile lend you thus much moneyes .

- at first it seems as if Shylocke is maintaining self-control: the first F sentence is only slightly passionately released (3/2 in five lines): then this is undercut by a more emotional second F sentence (1/4 in just three lines)

- then in F #3 emotional hell breaks loose with no fewer than twelve long spellings in just six lines

- even more dangerous is the sudden sense of control in the very short and unembellished sentences #4 (which is also monosyllabic) and #5

- and the danger seems to carry through into F's onrushed sentence #6 (split into two by most modern texts) with its opening surround phrase and icy calm broken by just two potentially very self-demeaning sarcastic long spelled words ('curre' and 'humblenesse'): then in the speech's last four lines Shylocke suddenly explodes via the overly-long shaded line (twelve syllables as shown, reset as a normal line plus pause by most modern texts) followed by four heavy pieces of punctuation in three lines (as opposed to only three in the previous nineteen)

this cluster has a double effect

- first, it's as if his mind is suddenly bursting, overflowing, with a series of powerful thoughts too strong to reign in—especially when two of the four are emotional semicolons

- second, the thoughts themselves are shown as five most unusual successive surround phrases ending the speech, as such all revealing the depth of his anger and hate,

  > ":Faire sir, you spet on me on Wednesday last ;/You spurn'd me such a day ;another time/You cald me dog : and for these curtesies/Ile lend you thus much moneyes ."

The Merchant of Venice

Anthonio

Marke you this Bassanio,
between 1.3.97—102 1.3.132–137

Background: not having the money to loan Bassanio immediately to hand, Anthonio has given him free rein to borrow from whomever he can. Unwittingly, Bassanio has contacted Shylocke, a man with whom Anthonio shares a reciprocal loathing and contempt. Much of this is based on the fact that Shylocke charges interest for the money that he lends, a condition Anthonio abhors. The following springs from the attempt Shylocke has just made to justify charging interest by quoting a supposed parallel from the bible, that of Jacob, Laban, and the sheep.

Style: as part of a three-handed scene

Where: unspecified

To Whom: Bassanio, perhaps as an aside or perhaps for Shylocke to hear

# of Lines: 12

Probable Timing: 0.40 minutes

Take Note: The extra spellings of the F text reveals it to be a very personally emotional speech, though the opening F clues are more than somewhat gutted by the tidiness of the modern resetting, especially creating a second sentence at the end of F #1's second line.

Antonio

1   Mark you this, Bassanio,
    The devil can cite Scripture for his purpose .

2   An evil soul producing holy witness
    Is like a villain with a smiling cheek,
    A goodly apple rotten at the heart .

3   O, what a goodly outside falsehood hath .

---

4   If thou wilt lend this money, lend it not
    As to thy friends, for when did friendship take
    A breed of barren metal of his friend ?

5   But lend it rather to thine enemy,
    Who if he break, thou mayst with better face
    Exact the [penalty] .

Anthonio

1   Marke you this Bassanio,
     The divell can cite Scripture for his purpose,
     An evill soule producing holy witnesse,
     Is like a villaine with a smiling cheeke,
     A goodly apple rotten at the heart .

2   O what a goodly outside falsehood hath .

---

3   If thou wilt lend this money, lend it not
     As to thy friends, for when did friendship take
     A breede of barraine mettall of his friend ?

4   But lend it rather to thine enemie,
     Who if he breake, thou maist with better face
     Exact the [penalties] .

- the larger of the two explosions comes at the start of the speech, where not only is the onrushed F #1 (split in two by modern texts) but most of the speech's emotional release is found in the first four lines (0/7), all of it concentrating on Anthonio's view of Shylocke as something inherently wicked ('divell', 'evill soule', 'villaine')

- however, in expressing his own hatred of pretence ('what a goodly outside falsehood hath') and that Shylocke shouldn't believe he is lending money 'to thy friends', it does seem that Anthonio has managed to calm himself, for by the last line of F #1, through F #2 and the opening of F #3, all excesses have disappeared, but this is only temporary for…

- … another explosion is released (0/3 in one line) when Anthonio describes friendship as never stooping to usury, 'A breede of barraine mettall', (which was destroying contemporary English landed families at the time the play was written)

- and then apparent public self control returns to end the speech (0/1, F #4)

The Merchant of Venice
Shylock/Jew

Jaylor, looke to him, tell not me of mercy,
between 3.3.1–18

Background: this is the first appearance of Shylocke since his avowal to his friend Tubal that as regards Anthonio 'I will have the heart of him if he forfeit', and, presumably, his first sight of Anthonio at large since Anthonio's imprisonment for debt. As such, the following is self explanatory.

Style: as part of a four handed scene

Where: unspecified, somewhere in the public view

To Whom: a Jaylor accompanying Anthonio, and Anthonio himself who is accompanied by his friend Solanio

# of Lines: 16

Probable Timing: 0.50 minutes

Take Note: When last seen with the taunting Christians and Tuball the Q/F prefix was the personal 'Shy.'. Now, in public, the Q/F prefix names him 'Jew', a prefix he keeps until the first signs of defeat in the trial scene. Q2 and most modern texts use 'Shy.' throughout and thus lose the transition in public persona. This is of even more concern when coupled with the modern text determination to show Shylocke still capable of dignified debate, which here leads them to expand F's onrushed five sentences into eleven short self-controlled rational statements—somewhat surprising when F's orthography shows the speech as emotional rather than intellectual (3/14 overall).

Shylock

1   Jailer, look to him, tell not me of mercy .

2   This is the fool that [lent] out money gratis .

3   Jailer, look to him .

---

4   I'll have my bond, speak not against my bond,
I have sworn an oath that I will have my bond .

5   Thou call'dst me dog before thou hadst a cause,
But since I am a dog, beware my fangs.

6   The Duke shall grant me justice .

7   I do wonder,
Thou naughty jailer, that thou art so fond
To come abroad with him at his request .

---

8   I'll have my bond; I will not hear thee speak.

9   I'll have my bond, and therefore speak no more .

10 I'll not be made a soft and dull-ey'd fool
To shake the head, relent, and sigh, and yield
To Christian intercessors .

11   Follow not,
I'll have no speaking, I will have my bond .

Jew

1   Jaylor, looke to him, tell not me of mercy,
     This is the foole that [lends] out money gratis .

2   Jaylor, looke to him .

---

3   Ile have my bond, speake not against my bond,
     I have sworne an oath that I will have my bond :
     Thou call'dst me dog before thou hadst a cause,
     But since I am a dog, beware my phangs,
     The Duke shall grant me justice, I do wonder
     Thou naughty Jaylor, that thou art so fond
     To come abroad with him at his request .

---

4   Ile have my bond, I will not heare thee speake,
     Ile have my bond, and therefore speake no more .

5   Ile not be made a soft and dull ey'd foole,
     To shake the head, relent, and sigh, and yeeld
     To Christian intercessors : follow not,
     Ile have no speaking, I will have my bond .

- throughout F, there is a greater spontaneous flow and immediacy: the frequent quick-link comma connections (reset as periods by most modern texts for mt. #5,#6 and #8, and then with more periods replacing the F colons mt. #4 and #10) suggest a mind working far more quickly than its modern counterpart

- yet, startlingly, within this onrush and the sudden bursts of emotion, the previously seen non-embellished and controlled Shylocke moments (speeches #18-21) are even more magnified here, with such supposedly emotive phrases as

  "Ile have my bond"—no fewer than three separate times!

  "Thou call'dst me dog before thou hadst a cause, /But since I am a dog"

  "The Duke shall grant me justice,"

  "I do wonder…that thou art so fond /To come abroad with him at his request."

  "follow not,…I will have my bond"

  all being uttered with no embellishment whatsoever, suggesting a very dangerous calm, especially given the circumstances

- within this calm there are occasional small powerful bursts of emotion, such as 'Jaylor, looke to him' twice, and 'I will not heare thee speake', but apart from these and the reference to his own 'phangs' and Anthonio as a 'foole' the sense of vocal control, even while the flow of the speech almost runs away with him, is quite remarkable

The Merchant of Venice

Anthonio

But little : I am arm'd and well prepar'd .
4.1.264–281

Background: Shylocke has not been dissuaded to abandon what seems to be legally his, the pound of his own flesh that Anthonio owes him. Thus Anthonio has been asked if he has anything to say before the execution of the terms of the bond, which would inevitably cause Anthonio's death, be carried out.

Style: one on one, with occasional playing for the much larger group also present

Where: the room/court where the hearing to gratify Shylocke's bond is being held

To Whom: primarily Bassanio, in front of the Duke, Gratiano, Shylocke, the legal team appearing to defend Anthonio (the unrecognised and disguised Portia and Nerrissa), court officials, and possibly friends and supporters of both parties

# of Lines: 18

Probable Timing: 0.55 minutes

Take Note: While the modern texts maintain Anthonio's dignity throughout, F shows key moments when his personal feelings momentarily break through.

Antonio

1   But little ; I am arm'd and well prepar'd .

2   Give me your hand, Bassanio, fare you well .

3   Grieve not that I am fall'n to this for you ;
    For herein fortune shows herself more kind
    Then is her custom .

4   It is still her use
    To let the wretched man outlive his wealth,
    To view with hollow eye and wrinkled brow
    An age of poverty ; from which ling'ring penance
    Of such misery doth she cut me off .

5   Commend me to your honorable wife,
    Tell her the process of Antonio's end,
    Say how I lov'd you, speak me fair in death ;
    And when the tale is told, bid her be judge
    Whether Bassanio had not once a love .

6   Repent [but] you that you shall loose your friend,
    And he repents not that he pays your debt ;
    For if the Jew do cut but deep enough,
    I'll pay it instantly with all my heart .

Anthonio

1   But little : I am arm'd and well prepar'd .

2   Give me your hand Bassanio, fare you well .

3   Greeve not that I am falne to this for you :
For heerein fortune shewes her selfe more kinde
Then is her custome .

4　　　　　　　　　　　It is still her use
To let the wretched man out-live his wealth,
To view with hollow eye, and wrinkled brow
An age of poverty .

5　　　　　　　　　From which lingring penance
Of such miserie, doth she cut me off :
Commend me to your honourable Wife,
Tell her the processe of Anthonio's end :
Say how I lov'd you ; speake me faire in death :
And when the tale is told, bid her be judge,
Whether Bassanio had not once a Love :
Repent [not] you that you shall loose your friend,
And he repents not that he payes your debt .

6   For if the Jew do cut but deepe enough,
Ile pay it instantly, with all my heart .

- the first moment of referring to death, no matter how obliquely (at the end of F #3) suddenly shows emotion for the first time in the speech (five long spelled words out of twelve in one and a half lines), and a further reference to death, at the start of F #5 is completely ungrammatical, and rarely followed by any modern text

- three of the five surround phrases occur as Anthonio finally begins to speak, no matter how obliquely, of his love for Bassanio

    " . Greeve not that I am falne to this for you : "

    " : Say how I lov'd you ; speake me faire in death : "

    yet, when attempting to console Bassanio, Anthonio manages to return to some (enforced?) dignified unembellished calm

- the end of the speech, where F #5 and #6 have been markedly re-shaped by modern texts, shows F Anthonio's control slip

    a. there is the totally ungrammatical period ending F #4, suggesting how desperately he needs a pause to establish self-control before he opens F #5 with an appearance of unembellished calm, which then jumps into passion (2/2) as he refers to what would forever be a rift between Anthonio and his hopes, Bassanio's new 'honourable Wife'

    b. there is F #5's ungrammatical onrush, with its five pieces of heavy punctuation in as many lines, suggesting that his mind is working much harder than his modern counterpart who maintains a much more grammatical, rational structure throughout

    c. and when he finally gets enough courage to make a public statement of his love for Bassanio, 'Whether Bassanio had not once a Love', it is so determinedly factual (2/0), yet he then plunges on ungrammatically via a colon (embarrassment for both of them, perhaps? or determination to prove how much he loves Bassanio) into the 'repent not' images, whereas modern texts create their tidy new sentence #6, reducing the impact of the blurt

- the value of F starting the new sentence (#6) when it does is that it emphasises the last line's wonderfully unembellished dignified wit in the face of death, 'Ile pay it instantly, with all my heart' (an attempt to recover from embarrassment again perhaps?)

Much Ado About Nothing

Leonato

Tush, tush, man, never fleere and jest at me,
between 5.1.58–79

Background: even though Hero is not dead, Leonato and the family must act as if she were. Having accidentally encountered Claudio and Don Pedro in the street, Leonato's anger gets the better of him, especially when insulted by Claudio who, in response to Leonato's comment 'Nay, never lay thy hand upon thy sword,/I feare thee not', offers the rather demeaning reply 'Marry beshrew my hand/If it should give your age such cause of feare,/Infaith my hand meant nothing to my sword.'

Style: part of a four-handed scene

Where: unspecified, presumably in a public place

To Whom: to Claudio, in front of Don Pedro and Leonato's brother Anthonio

# of Lines: 19

Probable Timing: 1.00 minutes

Take Note: When faced with a very disturbing emotional situation, rather than ranting off in all directions F shows Leonato, the wronged Hero's father, struggling between bursts of passion and attempts, via the unembellished lines, at self-control.

Leonato

1　Tush, tush, man, never fleer and jest at me ;
　I speak not like a dotard nor a fool,
　As under privilege of age to brag
　What I have done being young, or what would do
　Were I not old .

2　　　　　　　Know, Claudio, to thy head,
　Thou hast so wrong'd [mine] innocent child and me
　That I am forc'd to lay my reverence by,
　And with grey hairs and bruise of many days,
　Do challenge thee to trial of a man .

3　I say thou hast belied mine innocent child!

4　Thy slander hath gone through and through her heart
　And she lies buried with her ancestors -
　O, in a tomb where never scandal slept,
　Save this of hers, fram'd by thy villainy!

5　I'll prove it on {your} body, if {you} dare,
　Despite {your} nice fence and {your} active practice,
　{Your} May of youth and bloom of lustihood .

---

6 {†}　　　　　　　Thou hast kill'd my child .

7　If thou kill'st me, boy, thou shalt kill a man .

Leonato

1   Tush, tush, man, never fleere and jest at me,
    I speake not like a dotard, nor a foole,
    As under priviledge of age to bragge,
    What I have done being yong, or what would doe,
    Were I not old, know Claudio to thy head,
    Thou hast so wrong'd [my] innocent childe and me,
    That I am forc'd to lay my reverence by,
    And with grey haires and bruise of many daies,
    Doe challenge thee to triall of a man,
    I say thou hast belied mine innocent childe .

2   Thy slander hath gone through and through her heart,
    And she lies buried with her ancestors :
    O in a tombe where never scandall slept,
    Save this of hers, fram'd by thy villanie .

3   Ile prove it on {your} body if {you} dare,
    Despight {your} nice fence, and {your} active practise,
    {Your} Maie of youth, and bloome of lustihood .

---

4 {†}   Thou hast kild my child,
    If thou kilst me, boy, thou shalt kill a man .

- the unembellished lines speak as to from where Leonato's words and would-be actions stem: initially

  "…I am forc'd to lay my reverence by,"

  followed by the very long extended passage, much of F #2-4,

  "Thy slander hath gone through and through her heart,/And she lies buried with her ancestors:…, fram'd by thy villanie. / Ile prove it on {your} body if {you} dare,…/Thou hast kild my child,/If thou kilst me, boy, thou shalt kill a man."

- thus the opening scornful scolding of Claudio starts emotionally (0/3, the first thee lines): then Leonato seems to recover as he formally condemns Claudio for wronging 'my innocent childe and me' (1/2 the next four lines), but this does not last and he reverts to emotion as the formal challenge is made (0/4 the last three lines of F #1)

- and while F #2's opening two lines spelling out exactly what Claudio's 'slander' has done are unembellished, the notion of the 'scandall' it has brought to Leonato's family becomes emotional once more (0/2 the last two lines of F #2)

- the repetition of the invitation to fight (F #3-4) starts and finishes with great unembellished self-control, though the dismissal of Claudio's youthful strength becomes a mix of passion (1/2, the last two lines of F #3) and attempted control via short spellings 'villanie', 'Maie', 'kild', and 'kilst'

The Merry Wives of Windsor
Sir Hugh Evans

There is also another device in my praine,
between 1.1.43–57

Background: one of the first major speeches from the Welsh parson, also known as Sir Hugh. As a marriage-making proposal it is self-explanatory.

Style: as part of a three-handed scene

Where: somewhere close to the Page's home

To Whom: to Justice Shallow, the uncle of the proposed bridegroom, and the possible groom Abraham Slender

# of Lines: 11

Probable Timing: 0.40 minutes

Take Note: It seems that Evans cannot keep his outward calm for very long, for after the very restrained opening mention of a 'device in my praine' (0/1, F #1), excitement takes over.

Evans

1   {T}here is also another device in my prain, which
peradventure prings goot discretions with it : there is
Anne Page, which is daughter to Master [George] Page,
which is pretty virginity {,}

{a}s just as
you will desire, and seven hundred pounds of moneys,
and gold, and silver, is her grandsire upon his death's-
bed, (Got deliver to a joyful resurrections!) give, when
she is able to overtake seventeen years old .

2   It were a
goot motion if we leave our pribbles and prabbles, and
desire a marriage between Master Abraham and Mistress
Anne Page .

Evans

1 {T}here is also another device in my praine, which
peradventure prings goot discretions with it .

2   There is
Anne Page, which is daughter to Master [Thomas] Page,
which is pretty virginity{,}

                                   {a}s just as
you will desire, and seven hundred pounds of Moneyes,
and Gold, and Silver, is her Grand-sire upon his deaths-
bed, (Got deliver to a joyfull resurrections) give, when
she is able to overtake seventeene yeeres old .

3   It were a
goot motion, if we leave our pribbles and prabbles, and
desire a marriage betweene Master Abraham, and
Mistris Anne Page .

- the naming of names of the proposed marriage is stuffed full of facts, up to and including the Grand-sire's legacy (9/1, the first five lines of F #2), while the excitement of the legacy coming into effect now that Anne is 'seventeene yeeres old' turns into emotion (0/2, F #2's last line)

- the fact that F sets up the first mention of the names as a separate sentence (F #2, while modern texts fold it into their opening), gives even more weight to the proposal, especially since…

- …after a very careful unembellished appeal for calm by being calm, 'It were a goot motion, if we leave our pribbles and prabbles, and desire a marriage…', the naming of names is made once more, and once more is handled highly factually (5/1, the last one and a half lines of F #3)

The Merry Wives of Windsor

Falstaffe

Want no Mistresse Ford (Master Broome
between 2.2.260–286

Background: believing Pistoll that Falstaffe will attempt to woo his
wife, Ford has come to Falstaffe's rooms (disguised as one Master
Brooke) to encourage him in the act, presumably to expose him
publicly for what he is, and perhaps his wife too. Since Falstaffe
is now being offered money to achieve what he already intends to
do, and, as he believes, already has an open invitation from Mistris
Ford to woo her, the following is joyously self-explanatory.

Style: as part of a two-handed scene

Where: Falstaffe's rooms

To Whom: Ford, disguised as Master Brooke

# of Lines: 18

Probable Timing: 0.55 minutes

Take Note: What with three sentences (instead of most modern
texts' twelve), the first of two onrushed sentences equaling ten
modern sentences, and at least thirteen surround phrases, it seems
Falstaffe's delusional enthusiasm knows no bounds.

Falstaff

1   Want no Mistress Ford, Master [Brook], you shall
want none .

2   I shall be with her (I may tell you) by her
own appointment; even as you came in to me, her assistant or go-between parted from me .

3   I say I shall be
with her between ten and eleven ; for at that time the
jealous rascally knave her husband will be forth .

4 {†}   (Poor cuckoldly
knave) {†} .

5   Yet I wrong him to call him poor .

6   They say
the jealous wittolly knave hath masses of money, for
the which his wife seems to me well-favor'd.

7   I will use
her as the key of the cuckoldly rogue's coffer, {†}

{†} mechanical salt-butter rogue !

8   I will
stare him out of his wits ; I will awe him with my cud-
gel; it shall hang like a meteor o'er the cuckold's horns.

9   Master [Brook], thou shalt know I will predominate o-
ver the peasant, and thou shalt lie with his wife .

10   Come
to me soon at night .

11   Ford's a knave, and I will aggra-
vate his style; thou, Master [Brooke], shalt know him for
knave, and cuckold .

12   Come to me soon at night .

Falstaffe

1   Want no Mistresse Ford(Master [Broome]) you shall
    want none :I shall be with her (I may tell you) by her
    owne appointment, even as you came in to me, her assi-
    stant, or goe-betweene, parted from me :I say I shall be
    with her betweene ten and eleven : for at that time the
    jealious-rascally-knave her husband will be forth :

      {†} (poore Cuckoldly
    knave){†} :yet I wrong him to call him poore :They say
    the jealous wittolly-knave hath masses of money, for
    the which his wife seemes to me well-favour'd :I will use
    her as the key of the Cuckoldly-rogues Coffer, {†}

  {†} mechanicall-salt-butter rogue ;I wil
    stare him out of his wits : I will awe-him with my cud-
    gell : it shall hang like a Meteor ore the Cuckolds horns :
    Master Broome, thou shalt know, I will predominate o-
    ver the pezant, and thou shalt lye with his wife .

2   Come
    to me soone at night :Ford's a knave, and I will aggra-
    vate his stile : thou(Master [Broome]) shalt know him for
    knave, and Cuckold .

3   Come to me soone at night .

- there are hardly any unembellished phrases, so to find within the first three lines the quiet of 'even as you came in to me, her assistant... parted from me' could suggest that Falstaffe can hardly believe his luck, especially when coupled with the intervening phrase describing Mistris Ford's assistant as doubly long-spelled 'goe-betweene'

- the line and a half brag starting the speech is intellectual (4/2) and, even though the capitals involved all refer to names, the speech needn't have started this way so the idea of an opening flourish still stands

- the next four and a half lines boasting of being with her 'by her owne appointment' 'betweene ten and eleven' when 'her husband will be forth' is out and out emotional (0/4)

- starting with 'poore Cuckoldly knave', dwelling on Ford's 'masses of money' and using Mistris Ford as 'the key' to the 'Coffer', right through to the triumphant belief 'I will predominate over the pezant' releases Falstaffe's passions to the full (8/10 in the remaining eight and a half lines of F #1)

- the totally surround phrase created F #2, promising to tell all that evening, becomes intellectual (4/2), again returning to the style of the boast opening the speech

- and the final monosyllabic short sentence, repeating the promise of telling all that evening, becomes emotional (0/1), Falstaffe envisioning a-plenty perhaps

The Merry Wives of Windsor
Falstaffe

Have I caught thee, my heavenly Jewell ?
between 3.3.43–74

Background: not knowing of the Ladies' secret agenda to entice him into a laundry basket and dump him into the river Thames, and thus believing he is there to court an interested Mistris Ford, Falstaffe begins his wooing blandishments, couched in flattering hyperbole (with modern texts' regarding the opening line as one taken from a contemporary song). One note: the speech has been created by removing most of Mistris Ford's responses.

Style: as part of a two-handed scene

Where: Fords' home

To Whom: Mistris Ford

# of Lines: 18

Probable Timing: 0.55 minutes

Take Note: Given Falstaffe's earlier enthusiasm this speech is surprisingly restrained—whether because he is a skilful wooer allowing in the early stages his images to do his work, or whether he is so out of practice he doesn't quite know how

Falstaff

1 "Have I caught thee, my heavenly jewel ? "

2   Why,
now let me die, for I have liv'd long enough .

3   This is the
period of my ambition .

4   O this blessed hour !

5 Mistress Ford, I cannot cog, I cannot prate, [Mistress]
Ford .

6   Now shall I sin in my wish :I would thy husband
were dead .

7   I'll speak it before the best lord, I would
make thee my lady .

8 I see how thine eye would emulate the diamond .

9   Thou
hast the right arch'd beauty of the brow that becomes
the ship-tire, the tire-valiant, or any tire of Venetian
admittance .

10   Thou wouldst make
an absolute courtier, and the firm fixture of thy foot
would give an excellent motion to thy [gait] in a semi-
circled farthingale .

11   Come, I
cannot cog and say thou art this and that, like a many
of these lispinghawthorn buds, that come like women
in men's apparel, and smell like Bucklersbury in simple time—I cannot, but I love thee, none but thee ;and
thou deserv'st it .

Falstaffe

1   Have I caught thee, my heavenly Jewell ?

2   Why
now let me die, for I have liv'd long enough :This is the
period of my ambition :O this blessed houre .

---

3   Mistris Ford, I cannot cog, I cannot prate ([Mist .]
Ford) now shall I sin in my wish ; I would thy Husband
were dead, Ile speake it before the best Lord, I would
make thee my Lady .

---

4   I see how thine eye would emulate the Diamond :Thou
hast the right arched-beauty of the brow, that becomes
the Ship-tyre, the Tyre-valiant, or any Tire of Venetian
admittance .

---

5   Thou wouldst make
an absolute Courtier, and the firme fixture of thy foote,
would give an excellent motion to thy[gate], in a semi-
circled Farthingale .

---

6   Come, I
cannot cog, and say thou art this and that, like a-manie
of these lisping-hauthorne buds, that come like women
in mens apparrell, and smell like Bucklers-berry in simple time : I cannot, but I love thee, none but thee ;and
thou deserv'st it

- here the few surround phrases (somewhat surprising both for character and play) underscore his wooing tactics, as in all of F #2 ('now let me die'); the opening of F #4 (likening her eye as a 'Diamond'); and the end of F #6—see the final • below

- there is a splendid quiet opening to the wooing, with only one released word breaking into the unembellished short F #1 and start of F #2, though it may be that Falstaffe considers that one word, the doubly emphasised 'Jewell' coupled with the descriptive 'heavenly' might be more than enough to start the softening up process

- and then, as he moves into high-attack onrushed mode (F's remaining four and a bit sentences, reset as nine in most modern texts), surprisingly the wooing becomes much more intellectual than emotional—even in wishing 'thy Husband were dead' and when praising her brow 'that would do grace to any form of 'Tyre', i.e. head-dress (14/4, the ending of F #2 and all of F #3-4, eight lines in all)

- but as the wooing becomes more overall praising (she would make 'an absolute Courtier') and intimately physical-specific ('thy foote'), so Falstaffe becomes at one and the same time more controlled yet passionate, which is continued into the protestation that he 'cannot cog' (F #5 and the opening three and a half lines of F #6, just 3/4 in six and half lines)

- while the final two surround phrases unembellished declaration of love seems to be a wonderfully tricky piece of magnificent understatement, though Falstaffe does seem to lose his way at the last moment, for the excellent first phrases ' : . . but I love thee, none but thee ;' is more than somewhat undercut by the final self-aggrandizing ' ; and thou deserv'st it . '

The Merry Wives of Windsor

Falstaffe

Have I liv'd to be carried in a Basket
like a barrow of butchers Offal
3.5.4–18

Background: Falstaffe has not succeeded in seducing Mistris Ford, but she and Mistris Page do succeed in getting him to climb voluntarily into a laundry basket full of stinking clothes and then having their men stagger with it to the river and empty him into it—though their plan is almost scuppered by the unexpected arrival of Master Ford and friends before the basket leaves the home. Thus Falstaffe doesn't realise he's been punished by the women for daring to woo them, but rather believes they have in fact saved him from the wrath of a vengeful husband. The following deals with the river-dumping incident.

Style: solo

Where: Falstaffe's rooms

To Whom: direct audience address

# of Lines: 13

Probable Timing: 0.45 minutes

Take Note: Unusually both Folio and modern structures match, and, without F's usual onrush, Falstaffe seems to be in a much more contained mood, though whether he is relaxed as he talks to the audience as friends, or amazed at what has just occurred (or simply suffering from a chill) is up to each actor to decide.

Falstaff

1　Have I liv'd to be carried in a basket like a barrow of
butcher's offal! and to be thrown in the Thames ?

2　　　　　　　　　　　　　　　　　　　　　　　Well,
[and] I be serv'd such another trick, I'll have my brains
ta'en out and butter'd, and give them to a dog for a
new-year's gift .

3　　　　　　　　　The rogues slighted me into the river
with as little remorse, as they would have drown'd a
blind bitch's puppies, fifteen i'th litter ; and you may
know by my size, that I have a kind of alacrity in sinking ;
[and] the bottom were as deep as hell, I should down .

4　I had been drown'd, but that the shore was shelvy and
shallow—a death that I abhor ; for the water swells a
man ;and what a thing should I have been, when I
had been swell'd !

5　　　　　　　　　　　I should have been [a] mountain of
mummy .

Falstaffe

1   Have I liv'd to be carried in a Basket like a barrow of
    butchers Offall ? and to be throwne in the Thames ?

2   Wel,
    [if] I be serv'd such another tricke, Ile have my braines
    'tane out and butter'd, and give them to a dogge for a
    New-yeares gift .

3   The rogues slighted me into the river
    with as little remorse, as they would have drown'de a
    blinde bitches Puppies, fifteene i'th litter : and you may
    know by my size, that I have a kinde of alacrity in sinking :
    [if] the bottome were as deepe as hell, I shold down .

4   I had beene drown'd, but that the shore was shelvy and
    shallow : a death that I abhorre : for the water swelles a
    man ; and what a thing should I have beene, when I
    had beene swel'd ?

5   I should have beene [ ] Mountaine of
    Mummie .

- he opens quite passionately (3/2, the two lines of F #1) as he summarizes in surround phrases the double indignity of 'Have I liv'd to be carried in a Basket like a barrow of butchers Offall? and to be throwne in the Thames ? '

- and quite naturally the vow never to 'be serv'd such another tricke' becomes emotional (1/4, F #2)

- equally naturally remembering how he was 'slighted into the river', Falstaffe becomes very quiet, the recollection tinged with only a moment of passion (1/1, in the first three lines of F #3)

- and then the self-deprecating elaboration of how he has 'a kinde of alacrity in sinking' and he could drown even if 'the shore was shelvy and shallow', and what a sight he would be if he 'had beene swel'd', becomes emotional (0/7 in the remainder F #3 and F #4, six lines in all)—possibly Falstaffe's innate sense of story-teller's delight in direct audience address seen in Henry Four Parts One and Two has come to the fore once more, the whole underscored by being composed of six surround phrases

- and the short passionate F #5 (2/2) provides a wonderful flourish to the story

The Merry Wives of Windsor

Ford

Hum :ha ? Is this a vision ? Is this a dreame ?
3.5.138–152

Background: the disguised Ford's (hopeful?) question 'My suite then is desperate: You'll undertake her no more?' has triggered Falstaffe into making a defiant and triumphant claim to the contrary, based on the fact that Falstaffe genuinely believes he has been invited back by Mistris Ford that very morning to finish his as yet uncompleted wooing (not realising that she and Mistris Page are setting him up a second time). Unaware of his wife's plot with Mistris Page to lure Falstaffe to the house in order to punish him yet again, Ford is now even more convinced his wife is planning to have an affair.

Style: solo

Where: Falstaffe's rooms

To Whom: self, and direct audience address

# of Lines: 13

Probable Timing: 0.45 minutes

Take Note: F's orthography and especially sentence structure reveals a much more disturbed and perhaps uncontrolled Ford than most modern texts put forth.

Ford

1   Hum ! ha ?

2   Is this a vision ?

3   Is this a dream ?

4   Do I sleep ?

5   Master Ford, awake! awake, Master Ford !

6   There's a hole made in your best coat, Master Ford .

7   This
'tis to be married !

8   This 'tis to have linen, and buck-
baskets !

9   Well, I will proclaim myself what I am .

10 I will now take the lecher ; he is at my house .

11   He
cannot scape me ; 'tis impossible he should ; he cannot creep into a halfpenny purse, nor into a pepper
box .

12   But least the devil that guides him should
aid him, I will search impossible places .

13   Though
what I am I cannot avoid, yet to be what I would
not shall not make me tame .

14   If I have horns to make
one mad, let the proverb go with me : I'll be horn-
mad .

Ford

1   Hum : ha ?

2   Is this a vision ?

3   Is this a dreame ?
     doe I sleepe ?

4   Master Ford awake, awake Master Ford :
     ther's a hole made in your best coate(Master Ford :) this
     'tis to be married ; this 'tis to have Lynnen, and Buck-
     baskets : Well, I will proclaime my selfe what I am :
     I will now take the Leacher : hee is at my house :hee
     cannot scape me : 'tis impossible hee should : hee can-
     not creepe into a halfe-penny purse, nor into a Pepper-
     Boxe :But least the Divell that guides him, should
     aide him, I will search impossible places :though
     what I am, I cannot avoide ; yet to be what I would
     not, shall not make me tame :If I have hornes, to make
     one mad, let the proverbe goe with me, Ile be horne-
     mad .

- though Ford's opening matches in both texts, and the first two very short sentences are unembellished, suggesting a great deal of control, it is only momentarily, for the short F #3 self-questioning 'Is this a dreame?' becomes highly emotional (0/3)

- and the painful answer becomes one enormous onrush, (which most modern texts split into a rational progression of ten grammatically correct sentences), with at least eleven surround phrases

- the opening call to awake is totally intellectual (4/0, F #4's first line), and then, not surprisingly, the resulting attack on himself becomes very passionate (5/4 the next three and a half lines), all burnt into his imagination via four successive surround phrases, especially the emotional (semicolon created) ' : this 'tis to be married ; this 'tis to have Lynnen, and Buck-baskets : '

- however, the picturing of Falstaffe at his house and how he, Ford, will turn the place upside down to find him, and search even 'impossible places' becomes highly emotional (5/10 in the next four lines)

- the vow to not accept being a Cuckold is trebly enhanced, being expressed in two surround lines, one both monosyllabic, unembellished and formed in part by an emotional semicolon ': though what I am, I cannot avoide ; yet to be what I would not, shall not make me tame : '

- however, springing from that vow, the final resolution to be 'mad' becomes very emotional (1/4)

The Merry Wives of Windsor

Falstaffe

The Windsor-bell hath stroke twelve :
between 5.5.1–21

Background: incredibly, despite all that has happened, including a beating disguised as an old woman, Falstaffe still believes he has a chance with Mistris Ford. This time the women have tricked him to meet at midnight wearing, of all things, antlers on his head so as to follow their instruction to appear 'disguised like Herne with huge horns on his head'. Believing he will at last be successful, he shares his anticipation with the audience—little realising he is about to be exposed to everyone he has met in Windsor.

Style: initially solo, with the final two sentences to Mistris Ford

Where: at 'Herne the Hunter's Oake' in Windsor Forest

To Whom: direct audience address, and then Mistris Ford

# of Lines: 19

Probable Timing: 1.00 minutes

Take Note: Amazingly, the speech opens extraordinarily intellectually (20/3, F #1-2, and the first two and a half lines of F #3, just seven and a half lines in all), so it seems that Falstaffe is almost willing the help of the hot-blooded Gods, especially the king of all (Jove/Jupiter), and holding on to his emotional self very tightly so as not to deflect his literally horny plea.

Falstaff

1   The Windsor bell hath stroke twelve ; the mi-
nute drawson .

2   Now the hot-bloodied -gods assist me !

3   Remember, Jove, thou was't a bull for thy Europa, love
set on thy horns .

4   O powerful love, that in some respects
makes a beast a man ; in some other, a man a beast .

5   You were also, Jupiter, a swan, for the love of Leda .

6   O
omnipotent love, how near the god drew to the com-
plexion of a goose !

7   A fault done first in the form of a
beast (O Jove, a beastly fault !) and then another fault,
in the semblance of a fowl—think on't, Jove, a foul
fault !

8   When gods have hot backs, what shall poor
men do ?

9   For me, I am here a Windsor stag, and the
fattest, I think, i'th forest .

10   Send me a cool rut-time,
Jove, or who can blame me to piss my tallow ?

11   Who
comes here ?

---

12   My doe with the black scut ?

13   Let the sky
rain potatoes ; let it thunder to the tune of "Greensleeves", hailkissing comfits, and snow eringoes ; let
there come a tempest of provocation, I will shelter me
here.

Falstaffe

1　The Windsor-bell hath stroke twelve : the Mi-
nute drawes-on :Now the hot-bloodied -Gods assist me :
Remember Jove, thou was't a Bull for thy Europa, Love
set on thy hornes .

2　　　　　　　　　O powerfull Love, that in some respects makes a Beast a Man:in som other, a Man a beast .

3　You were also(Jupiter) a Swan, for the love of Leda :O
omnipotent Love, how nere the God drew to the com-
plexion of a Goose : a fault done first in the forme of a
beast, (O Jove, a beastly fault :) and then another fault,
in the semblance of a Fowle, thinke on't(Jove) a fowle-
fault .

4　　　　When Gods have hot backes, what shall poore
men do ?

5　　　　　For me, I am heere a Windsor Stagge, and the
fattest(I thinke) i'th Forrest .

6　　　　　　　　　Send me a coole rut-time
(Jove) or who can blame me to pisse my Tallow ?

7　　　　　　　　　　　　　　Who
comes heere ?

8　My Doe, with the blacke Scut ?

9　　　　　　　　Let the skie
raine Potatoes : let it thunder, to the tune of Greene-
sleeves, haile-kissing Comfits, and snow Eringoes: Let
there come a tempest of provocation, I will shelter mee
heere .

- despite the control, his need for success comes burning through both with the opening onrush (the two and a half sentences of F's intellectual opening being reset as seven by most modern texts) and the opening two lines of F #1, all of F #2, and the opening of F #3 being all surround phrases

- as ever, once Falstaffe starts to dream, so his passions or emotions come to the fore; and here is no exception, for as the lust begins to rise 'a fault done first the forme of a beast', so the remainder of the sentence turns passionate (4/4, the last three lines of F #3)

- and, as the short sentences continue the lust chat with the Gods, asking for a 'a coole rut-time' so that he doesn't 'pisse my Tallow', excusing himself for 'When Gods have hot backes, what shall poore men do?' (F #4-6), so the passions still run free (8/8 in just four lines)

- and as reality at last appears, so the passions disappear for a moment, with the two short sentences first becoming emotional ('Who comes heere?', 0/1) and then factual with his extremely vulgar acknowledgement of which lady has arrived ('My Doe, with the blacke Scut?', 2/1)

- and then, as he realises his dreams might at last come true, the delighted celebratory yell for what were then believed to be aphrodisiacs ('Potatoes' and the sweetmeats known as 'Eringoes') and a love-song (which 'Greensleeves' was reckoned to be), so passions have their full sway once more (4/4 in the three and a half lines of F #9)

As You Like It
Duke Senior

Now my Coe-mates, and brothers in exile :
2.1.1–17

Background: this is the first speech in the play for the exiled Duke Senior, spoken to some of his loyal followers who chose voluntary exile with him. Given that it is winter, the speech is self-explanatory. One note: the implication of 'Coe-mates', the compound noun in the opening line, suggests a social equality rarely seen in any other Shakespeare play save perhaps the 'Crispin-Crispian' speech of Henry V.

Style: group address

Where: at his encampment in the woods

To Whom: his followers, including Amyens

# of Lines: 17

Probable Timing: 0.55 minutes

Take Note: Given that the Duke is often played as a quiet academic, the relative lack of intellectual release in the following (either capitals or colons) may be somewhat surprising (7/24), and could suggest a much more complete man than seen in many productions.

Duke Senior

1   Now, my co-mates and brothers in exile,
     Hath not old custom made this life more sweet
     [Than] that of painted pomp ?

2   Are not these woods
     More free from peril [than] the envious court ?

3   Here feel we not the penalty of Adam,
     The season's difference, as the icy fang
     And churlish chiding of the winter's wind,
     Which when it bites and blows upon my body
     Even till I shrink with cold, I smile and say
     "This is no flattery : these are counsellors
     That feelingly persuade me what I am ."

4   Sweet are the uses of adversity,
     Which like the toad, ugly and venomous,
     Wears yet a precious jewel in his head ;
     And this our life, exempt from public haunt,
     Finds tongues in trees, books in the running brooks,
     Sermons in stones, and good in every thing

Duke Senior

1   Now my Coe-mates, and brothers in exile :
     Hath not old custome made this life more sweete
     [Then] that of painted pompe ?

2   Are not these woods
     More free from perill [then] the envious Court ?

3   Heere feele we not the penaltie of Adam,
     The seasons difference, as the Icie phange
     And churlish chiding of the winters winde,
     Which when it bites and blowes upon my body
     Even till I shrinke with cold, I smile, and say
     This is no flattery : these are counsellors
     That feelingly perswade me what I am :
     Sweet are the uses of adversitie
     Which like the toad, ougly and venemous,
     Weares yet a precious Jewell in his head :
     And this our life exempt from publike haunt,
     Findes tongues in trees, bookes in the running brookes,
     Sermons in stones, and good in every thing .

- given the enormously surprising non-hierarchical almost-communist-in its-equality content ('Coe-mates' and 'brothers'), it seems only right that the first line is both a surround line and intellectual, though, apart from the passion of F #2, this is virtually the only time intellect comes into any serious consideration throughout the speech

- the attempt to convince his followers of life in the woods being 'sweete' (despite it being winter!) is emotional (0/3, the last two lines of F #1)

- and, after the passionate question (or statement, given that the Elizabethan question mark could also function as a modern exclamation point) that at least the woods are less perilous than the 'envious Court' (1/1, F #2), the remaining justification that the hardships they are currently undergoing are 'Sweet' in their 'adversitie', and that in nature they find 'good in every thing', is almost completely emotional (3/13 in the thirteen lines of F #3)

- while the most telling point for the Duke may well be the only other surround phrase, as he tries to make good the 'churlish chiding' of the 'winters winde'

  " : these are counsellors/That feelingly perswade me what I am : "

As You Like It

Corin

{†} **I know the more one sickens, the worse at ease he is :**
3.2.23–31 plus 3.2.73–77

Background: Corin's response to Touchstone's blatant question, 'Has't any Philosophie in thee shepheard?'. One note: sentence F #3 originally followed Touchstone's teasing suggestion that Corin may be 'damn'd'– in the context of this speech the sentence could be triggered by supposed laughter from Corin's scene partner.

Style: as part of a two-handed scene

Where: somewhere in the woods, near the cottage of Rosalind and Celia

To Whom: Touchstone

# of Lines: 13

Probable Timing: 0.45 minutes

Take Note: The capital letters in the Folio highlight the main points of Corin's philosophy.

Corin

1 {†}　　　　　　　　　I know the more one sickens
the worse at ease he is ; and that he that wants money,
means, and content is without three good friends; that
the property of rain is to wet and fire to burn ; That
good pasture makes fat sheep; and that a great cause of
the night is lack of the Sun; that he that hath learned no wit by nature, nor art, may complain of good
breeding, or comes of a very dull kindred .

---

2 {†} I am a true laborer: I earn that I eat, get
that I wear, owe no man hate, envy no mans happi-
ness, glad of other men's good, content with my harm,
and the greatest of my pride, is to see my ewes graze &
　　　　　　　　　　　　　　　　　　my lambs suck .

Corin

1 {†}   I know the more one sickens,
the worse at ease he is : and that hee that wants money,
meanes, and content, is without three good frends .

2   That
the propertie of raine is to wet, and fire to burne : That
good pasture makes fat sheepe : and that a great cause of
the night, is lacke of the Sunne : That hee that hath learned no wit by Nature, nor Art, may complaine of good
breeding, or comes of a very dull kindred .

---

3 {†}   I am a true Labourer, I earne that I eate : get
that I weare ; owe no man hate, envie no mans happi-
nesse ; glad of other mens good content with my harme :
and the greatest of my pride, is to see my Ewes graze, &
                                                    my Lambes sucke .

- That perhaps Corin only eventually finds a way to triumph in his 'Philosophie' might be seen in the build—first F #1's quiet start with four of six phrases being unembellished; then the growth first to emotion (0/5, F #1 and the first two lines of F #2); and then the moment of slight passion(1/1 in one line) over 'night' being caused by 'the lacke of the Sunne', which leads to his final much more passionate two line flourish with its sly dig at 'good breeding' (3/2 F #2).

- That this starts as hard work for him might be seen in the five surround phrases/lines that open the speech, and the two extra breath-thoughts by which he strains to add the necessary extra detail to the point being made.

- However, his strong self-definition of F #3 is a very different matter, with emotion flowing from the very start (1/6 in the first three lines), the emotion further heightened with three of the five surround phrases formed in part by the emotional semicolons.

- Thus it's interesting to see the (dignified?) ending as he describes his greatest pride (2/1, the last line and a half).

Twelfe Night, or, what you will
Malvolio

To be Count Malvolio .
between 2.5.35–80

Background: Maria has dropped the Malvolio-enticing letter, written in exact copy of Olivia's handwriting, and he is about to discover it. Believing he is alone he indulges in his, presumably favourite, fantasy. In fact Toby, Andrew and Fabian (not Feste as originally suggested) are hidden in the box-trees watching his every move, listening to his every word. One note, the speech is constructed by removing all the sotto voce asides between Toby, Andrew, and Fabian.

Style: solo, in front of three very interested eaves-droppers

Where: somewhere in Olivia's gardens

To Whom: self, and audience, in front of the hidden Toby, Andrew and Fabian

# of Lines: 22

Probable Timing: 1.10 minutes

Take Note: That the hopes of marrying Olivia are such an essential part of Malvolio's psyche can be seen in the short sentences that open and, especially, close the speech; the fact that there is no consistency in release from one sentence to the next; and the content of the surround phrases.

Malvolio

1   To be Count Malvolio ! {†}

2   There is example for't ; the Lady of the Strachy, married the yeoman of the wardrobe .{†}

3   Having been three months married to her,
sitting in my state—{†}

4   Calling my officers about me, in my branch'd
velvet gown; having come from a day-bed, where I
have left Olivia sleeping—{†}

5   And then to have the humor of state ; and after
a demure [travel] of regard—telling them I know my
place as I would they should do theirs—to ask for
my kinsman Toby—{†}

6   Seven of my people with an obedient start,
make out for him .

7   I frown the while, and perchance
wind up my watch, or play with my—some rich jewel.

8   Toby approaches ; curtsies there to me—{†}

9   I extend my hand to him thus, quenching my
familiar smile with an austere regard of control—{†}

10 Saying, "Cousin Toby, my fortunes, having cast
me on your niece, give me this prerogative of
speech"—{†}

11 "You must amend your drunkenness.{†}

12 "Besides, you waste the treasure of your time,
with a foolish knight—{†}

13 One Sir Andrew ."{†}

Malvolio

1   To be Count Malvolio . {†}

2   There is example for't : The Lady of the Stra-
    chy, married the yeoman of the wardrobe .{†}

3   Having beene three moneths married to her,
    sitting in my state .{†}

4   Calling my Officers about me, in my branch'd
    Velvet gowne : having come from a day bedde, where I
    have left Olivia sleeping .{†}

5   And then to have the humor of state : and after
    a demure [travaile] of regard : telling them I knowe my
    place, as I would they should doe theirs : to aske for
    my kinsman Toby .{†}

6   Seaven of my people with an obedient start,
    make out for him : I frowne the while, and perchance
    winde up my watch, or play with my some rich Jewell :
    Toby approaches ; curtsies there to me .{†}

7   I extend my hand to him thus : quenching my
    familiar smile with an austere regard of controll .{†}

8   Saying, Cosine Toby, my Fortunes having cast
    me on your Neece, give me this prerogative of
    speech .{†}

9   You must amend your drunkennesse .{†}

10 Besides you waste the treasure of your time,
    with a foolish knight .{†}

11 One sir Andrew .{†}

- F #2's first surround phrase focuses on his need to find a parallel on which he can build his hopes

  " There is example for't : The Lady of the Strachy, married the yeoman of the wardrobe . "

  heightened by the first phrase being monosyllabic and unembellished, and the second (naturally with the naming of names, 3/0) deeply factual

- and then, startlingly, in one of the most extended sequences of such phrases in the canon, the next eleven imagination lines reeking of images of power and eroticism are formed by twelve successive surround phrases (F #4-7), the most powerful of all seeming to be the humiliation of Toby, as the semicolon created surround phrases show

  " : Toby approaches ; curtsies there to me . "

- Malvolio starts out highly intellectually (5/0, F #1-2), the opening short sentence shows where the dream is focused—not on Olivia herself, but on the status marrying her will give him, though the idea of three months married to her is momentarily emotional (0/2, F #3)

- and, as the dreams of 'Calling my Officers about me' (F #4) and the later extension into 'Seaven of my people' to go get Toby (F #6) takes shape (and note the long-spelling of 'Seaven'), so the passions flow (3/2 and 2/3, respectively), while the scolding of them (F #5) is splendidly emotional (1/5)

- however, the scolding of Toby, after a moment of emotion (F #7, 0/1, delight perhaps), is initially highly intellectual (4/1, F #8)

- and then it seems some sort of mask drops, and Malvolio ends much more directly with two short sentences out of three, Toby's 'drunkennesse' handled emotionally (0/1) while Andrew is initially icily dismissed (the unembellished F #10) and then factually (1/0, F #11), the little regard Malvolio has for him shown in the fact that Andrew's title is not capitalized

Twelfe Night, or, what you will
Malvolio

Oh ho, do you come neere me now : no worse
3.4.64–83

Background: Malvolio has done everything the letter has commanded
to excess, and of course Olivia now doubts his sanity. Unfortunately
Olivia's final words as she makes a hasty exit to meet with Cesario
once more, 'Where's my Cosine Toby, let some of my people have a
speciall care of him, I would not have him miscarrie for the halfe of
my Dowry'—the 'him' referring to Malvolio—only seems to convince him of the veracity of the letter, and inflame him even more.

Style: solo

Where: somewhere in Olivia's home

To Whom: direct audience address

# of Lines: 19

Probable Timing: 1.00 minutes

Malvolio

1   O ho, do you come near me now ?

2   No worse
man [than] Sir Toby to look to me !

3   This concurs directly with the letter : she sends him on purpose, that I may
appear stubborn to him ; for she incites me to that in
the letter .

4   "Cast thy humble slough," says she ; be oppo-
site with a kinsman, surly with servants ; let thy tongue
[tang] with arguments of state; put thyself into the
trick of singularity"; and consequently sets down the
manner how : as a sad face, a reverend carriage, a slow
tongue, in the habit of some sir of note, and so forth .

5   I have lim'd her, but it is Jove's doing, and Jove make me
thankful!

6   And when she went away now, "Let this fellow be look'd too"; "fellow" ! not "Malvolio", nor after my
degree, but "fellow" .

7   Why, every thing adheres together,
that no dram of a scruple, no scruple of a scruple, no
obstacle, no incredulous or unsafe circumstance—What
can be said ?

8   Nothing that can be, can come between
me, and the full prospect of my hopes .

9   Well, Jove, not I,
is the doer of this, and he is to be thank'd .

Malvolio

1   Oh ho, do you come neere me now : no worse
man [then] sir Toby to looke to me .

2   This concurres directly with the Letter, she sends him on purpose, that I may
appeare stubborne to him : for she incites me to that in
the Letter .

3   Cast thy humble slough sayes she : be oppo-
site with a Kinsman, surly with servants, let thy tongue
[langer] with arguments of state, put thy selfe into the
tricke of singularity : and consequently setts downe the
manner how : as a sad face, a reverend carriage, a slow
tongue, in the habite of some Sir of note, and so foorth .

4   I have lymde her, but it is Joves doing, and Jove make me
thankefull .

5   And when she went away now, let this Fellow be look'd too : Fellow ? not Malvolio, nor after my
degree, but Fellow .

6   Why every thing adheres togither,
that no dramme of a scruple, no scruple of a scruple, no
obstacle, no incredulous or unsafe circumstance : What
can be saide ?

7   Nothing that can be, can come betweene
me, and the full prospect of my hopes .

8   Well Jove, not I,
is the doer of this, and he is to be thanked .

- once more the surround phrases highlight the most fervent of Malvolio's hopes

    " . Oh ho, do you come neere me now : no worse man then sir Toby to looke to me . "

    " : for she incites me to that in the Letter . Cast thy humble slough sayes she : "

    " : and consequently setts downe the manner how : "

    " . And when she went away now, let this Fellow be look'd too : Fellow ? not Malvolio, nor after my degree, but Fellow ."

    " : What can be saide ? "

- with his new 'tricke of singularity' seeming to have worked better than he could have hoped, the speech starts emotionally (1/3, F #1)

- that this agrees with the 'Letter' (capitalised twice) becomes passionate (F #2, 2/3), and as Malvolio continues to remind himself of what the letter told him to do, he becomes emotional once more (2/7, F #3)

- with the notion that he has 'lymde her' having to be swiftly turned into 'Jove'/God's doing and not his, his passions come to the fore (2/2, the short F #4)

- the determination to turn anything into proof positive of Olivia's love has him transpose the rather dismissive 'Fellow' into something worthwhile and has his mind working to the exclusion of all else (4/0, F #5)

- and after this, as with the previous speech, though still essentially emotional as he realises 'every thing adheres togither' and again thanks 'Jove', his energy, or at least his releases, seem to diminish once more (1/3, the five lines ending the speech, F #6-8)

Alls Well that Ends Well

Clowne

I hope to have friends for my wives sake,
between 1.3.39–63

Background: the Countesse has kept on Lavatch, a clown belonging to her late husband. Blessed with a mordant wit, here he offers a somewhat cynical view of marriage, and the apparent benefits in having a wife who may cheat on him.

Style: as part of a two-handed scene

Where: somewhere in the palace of Rossillion

To Whom: the Countesse

# of Lines: 17

Probable Timing: 0.55 minutes

Take Note: While most modern texts set up a highly rational six sentence character, thus implying that Lavatch's wit is well under control, and that he finishes neatly and tidily with a ballad. However, F's two onrushed sentences plus his speaking in rhyme rather than singing it suggests a much more challenged, challenging, and sardonic character. Compared to the following speech, it seems Lavatch finds either the subject of marriage, or amusing the Countesse, one of his more difficult tasks.

Clown

1   I hope to have friends for my wive's sake ,

---

                                                    for the
knaves come to do that for me which I am a weary of .

2   He that ears my land spares my team, and gives me
leave to inn the crop .

3   If I be his cuckold he's my
drudge .

4   He that comforts my wife is the cherisher of
my flesh and blood ; he that cherishes my flesh and
blood loves my flesh and blood ; he that loves my flesh
and blood is my friend : ergo, he that kisses my wife is my
friend .

5   If men could be contented to be what they are,
there were no fear in marriage, for young Charbon the
puritan and old Poysam the papist, how some'er their
hearts are sever'd in religion, their heads are both one :
they may jowl horns together like any deer i'th'herd .

---

6   A prophet I, {†} and I speak the truth, {†}
                For I the ballad will repeat,
               Which men full true shall find:
               Your marriage comes by destiny,
                Your cuckoo sings by kind .

Clowne

1   I hope to have friends for my wives sake ,

---

                                              for the
knaves come to doe that for me which I am a wearie of :
he that eres my Land, spares my teame, and gives mee
leave to Inne the crop : if I be his cuckold hee's my
drudge ; he that comforts my wife, is the cherisher of
my flesh and blood ; hee that cherishes my flesh and
blood, loves my flesh and blood ; he that loves my flesh
and blood is my friend : ergo, he that kisses my wife is my
friend : if men could be contented to be what they are,
there were no feare in marriage, for yong Charbon the
Puritan, and old Poysam the Papist, how somere their
hearts are sever'd in Religion, their heads are both one,
they may joule horns together like any Deare i'th Herd .

---

2   A Prophet I, {†} and I speake the truth, {†}
for I the Ballad will repeate, which men full
true shall finde, your marriage comes by destinie, your
Cuckow sings by kinde .

- as with several of Shakespeare's Clowne/Foole's (notably Touchstone), Lavatch begins deceptively calmly in setting up the premise from which the ensuing wit games will stem (0/1 the first two lines)

- and then begins a series of mildly emotional chop-logic embellishments on the theme of a man's wife's infidelity having its own rewards (2/5, in the seven and a half lines till the final colon of the speech), here highly overworked in being set as six consecutive surround phrases, with the most highly cynical points within the argument underscored by three successive emotional semicolons, viz.

  " : if I be his cuckold hee's my drudge ; he that comforts my wife, is the cherisher of my flesh and blood ; hee that cherishes my flesh and blood, loves my flesh and blood ; he that loves my flesh and blood is my friend :"

- and once the foolishness of the final surround phrase ' : ergo, he that kisses my wife is my friend : ' is over, so Lavatch becomes highly intellectual in the put down of both Protestants and Catholics alike (7/3, the last five lines of F #1)

- and the F spoken rather than sung jaundiced maxim that ends the speech (as shown by the shaded lines) becomes emotionally passionate (3/5, F #2) thus matching the surround phrase elaborations offered earlier

Alls Well that Ends Well

Clowne

Why sir, if I cannot serve you, I can serve
between 4.5.36–55

Background: the King and his entourage are staying with the Countess at Rossilion, for the King plans to make peace with Bertram, and, believing Hellen to have died, as everyone now does, is intending to arrange a new marriage between Bertram and Lafew's daughter. Lafew, in accompanying the King, has had some private words with the Countesse, and then attempts to exchange wits with Lavatch, who (whether seriously or no) counters with the following once Lafew has refused Lavatch's original offer to be 'At your service' with a resounding 'No, no, no.'

Style: as part of a three-handed scene

Where: somewhere in the palace or grounds of Rossillion

To Whom: Lafew, in front of the Countesse

# of Lines: 13

Probable Timing: 0.45 minutes

Take Note: As with the previous speech, Lavatch starts quietly. However, whereas the previous speech was quite heavily released (12/14 in sixteen and a half lines), the discussion of his relationship with the dark forces is handled more carefully (5/9 in thirteen lines).

Clown

1   Why, sir, if I cannot serve you, I can serve as
     great a prince as you are .

---

2   'A has an English [name],
     but his fisnomy is more hotter in France [than] there .

---

3   The black prince, sir, alias the prince of darkness,
     alias the devil .

---

4   I am a woodland fellow, sir, that always lov'd
     a great fire, and the master I speak of ever keeps a good
     fire .

5   But sure he is the prince of the world ; let his no-
     bility remain in's court .

6   I am for the house with the
     narrow gate, which I take to be too little for pomp to
     enter .

7   Some that humble themselves may, but the ma-
     ny will be too chill and tender, and they'll be for the
     flow'ry way that leads to the broad gate and the great
     fire .

Clowne

1   Why sir, if I cannot serve you, I can serve as
    great a prince as you are .

---

2   'A has an English [maine],
    but his fisnomie is more hotter in France [then] there .

---

3   The blacke prince sir, alias the prince of darkenesse,
    alias the divell .

---

4   I am a woodland fellow sir, that alwaies loved
    a great fire, and the master I speake of ever keeps a good
    fire, but sure he is the Prince of the world, let his No-
    bilitie remaine in's Court .

5   I am for the house with the
    narrow gate, which I take to be too little for pompe to
    enter : some that humble themselves may, but the ma-
    nie will be too chill and tender, and theyle bee for the
    flowrie way that leads to the broad gate, and the great
    fire .

- after the unembellished premise as set up in F #1, Lavatch's first clue as to whom the 'great a prince' might be is slightly factual (2/1, F #2), and, as befits the entertainer, the naming of the 'divell' is accompanied by a total (and presumably surprising) change in style (0/3 in the short F #3)

- his self-description, and thus why he has a relationship with such a 'master', becomes passionate (3/2, F #4)

- and then, surprisingly, his further self-definition as being the entry presumably to heaven 'for the house with the narrow gate' (after all the supposed worship of the devil) and why, becomes very calm, suggesting an ease not seen in the previous speech, an admission of his true self perhaps (0/3, the four and a half lines of F #5), with two of the three releases (joyfully perhaps?) clustered together (viz. 'theyle bee') for those whose pride and self-deception ensures that they will go to hell

The Winter's Tale
Old Shepheard

I would there were no age betweene ten and . . .
3.3.59–78

Background: close to the spot where Antigonus abandoned the daughter of Leontes and Hermione, this is the first speech for the character, and as such it is self-explanatory.

Style: solo

Where: somewhere on the shores of Bohemia

To Whom: self, and direct audience address

# of Lines: 19

Probable Timing: 1.00 minutes

Take Note: The Old Shepheard seems to have an interesting style when something important occurs to him, for he often seems to conclue an idea, or push forward the start of a new one by means of surround phrases—as with his fury with the 'boylde-braines' young men whose hunting caused his sheep to stray (ending F #1); the knowledge of where his sheep might be (ending F #2)—possibly a pleasant realisation since it begins with an emotional ; F #5's discovery of the child; the fact that the child is not dressed warmly enough (the end of F #6); and the need for the advice of his son (all of F #7).

Old Shepheard

1   I would there were no age between ten and
three and twenty, or that youth would sleep out the rest ;
for there is nothing (in the between) but getting wen-
ches with child, wronging the ancientry, stealing,
fighting—hark you now !

2   Would any but these boil'd-
brains of nineteen and two and twenty hunt this wea-
ther ?

3   They have scar'd away two of my best sheep,
which I fear the wolf will sooner find [than] the master .

4   If any where I have them, 'tis by the seaside, brow-
ing of ivy .

5   Good luck, and't be thy will !

6   What have
we here ?

7   Mercy on's, a barne ?

8   A very pretty barne!

9   A
boy, or a child, I wonder ?

10   A pretty one, a very pretty
one : sure some scape .

11   Though I am not bookish, yet I
can read waiting-gentlewoman in the scape .

12   This has
been some stair-work, some trunk-work, some
behind-door work .

13   They were warmer that got this,
[than] the poor thing is here .

14   I'll take it up for pity, yet
I'll tarry till my son come ; he hallow'd but even now .

15 Whoa-ho-hoa .

Old Shepheard

1   I would there were no age betweene ten and
three and twenty, or that youth would sleep out the rest :
for there is nothing (in the betweene) but getting wen-
ches with childe, wronging the Auncientry, stealing,
fighting, hearke you now : would any but these boylde-
braines of nineteene, and two and twenty hunt this wea-
ther ?

2   They have scarr'd away two of my best Sheepe,
which I feare the Wolfe will sooner finde [then] the Mai-
ster ; if any where I have them, 'tis by the sea-side, brou-
zing of Ivy .

3   Good-lucke (and't be thy will) what have
we heere ?

4   Mercy on's, a Barne ?

5   A very pretty barne ; A
boy, or a Childe I wonder ?

6   (A pretty one, a verie prettie
one) sure some Scape ; Though I am not bookish, yet I
can reade Waiting-Gentlewoman in the scape : this has
beene some staire-worke, some Trunke-worke, some
behinde-doore worke : they were warmer that got this,
[then] the poore Thing is heere .

7   Ile take it up for pity, yet
Ile tarry till my sonne come : he hallow'd but even now .

8   Whoa-ho-hoa .

- Given the releases that come later in the speech, the relative calm in the first two lines (0/1) is surprising, and might suggest that the character is exhausted from looking for his missing sheep.

- But then comes the (traditional-old-man-complaining-about-the-young) emotional explosion at the young idiots who have caused two of his sheep to go missing (1/6, the last five lines of F #1).

- And though the facts of what has occurred and where he may find them then get added in, he still remains highly emotional (4/7, F #2).

- The initial discovery of what turns out to be the child is heightened by being both emotional (0/2, F #3) and set as the first of three successive short sentences, which then turns to passion (3/3, F #4-5) as he realises that what he has found is a baby—which seems to push him into a state of great calm (perhaps trying not to wake the child) for the first two unembellished closer examination phrases of F #6.

- And then, as he comes to believe that the child is a result of a 'Scape' by some 'Waiting-Gentlewoman', so he becomes intellectual (4/1, lines two and three of F #6), but this quickly turns into emotion as he elaborates on the 'behinde-doore worke' in the child's conception, and its lack of warm clothing (2/10 in the three lines ending F #6).

- After all the bluster, his decision to protect the child is very quietly taken (0/1, F #7), though F #8's apparent yell to his son may wake the baby up!

The Winter's Tale

Polixenes

Marke your divorce (yong sir)
between 4.4.417–441

Background: having struck up a conversation with Florizell (who still does not realise the stranger is his disguised father) about his intentions towards Perdita, and having failed to persuade his son to let his father know of his intentions, Polixines finally throws off his disguise and, as the following clearly shows, his anger knows no bounds.

Style: a four-hander in front of a larger group

Where: Bohemia, outdoors, where the sheep-shearing festival is to be held

To Whom: variously at times to his son Florizell, the Old Shepherd, and Perdita, in front of Camillo and whomever of the guests has remained on stage

# of Lines: 25

Probable Timing: 1.15 minutes

Take Note: Polixenes' quietness when making his most disturbing threats and judgments suggests a man who is very used to be listened to (as only befits a king), thus it's very interesting to see that most of the releases are directed, when they do come, towards his son primarily (especially when threatening to bar him from succession), and only rarely towards Perdita or her father.

Polixenes

1   Mark your divorce, young sir,
    Whom son I dare not call .

2   Thou art too base
    To be acknowledg'd .

3   Thou, a sceptre's heir,
    That thus affects a sheep-hook !

4   Thou, old traitor,
    I am sorry, that by hanging thee, I can
    But shorten thy life one week .

5   And thou, fresh piece
    Of excellent witchcraft, [who] of force must know
    The royal fool thou cop'st with—
    _____

    I'll have thy beauty scratch'd with briers & made
    More homely [than] thy state .

6   For thee, fond boy,
    If I may ever know thou dost but sigh
    That thou no more shalt [ ] see this knack (as never
    I mean thou shalt), we'll bar thee from succession,
    Not hold thee of our blood, no, not our kin,
    Far [than] Deucalion off .

7   Mark thou my words .

8   Follow us to the court .

9   Thou, churl, for this time,
    Though full of our displeasure, yet we free thee
    From the dead blow of it .

10   And you, enchantment—
    Worthy enough a herdsman , yea, him too,
    That makes himself (but for our honor therein)
    Unworthy thee—if ever, henceforth, thou
    These rural latches to his entrance open,
    Or [hoop] his body more with thy embraces,
    I will devise a death, as cruel for thee
    As thou art tender to't .

Polixenes

1   Marke your divorce(yong sir)
    Whom sonne I dare not call : Thou art too base
    To be acknowledged .

2   Thou a Scepters heire,
    That thus affects a sheepe-hooke ?

3   Thou, old Traitor,
    I am sorry, that by hanging thee, I can
    But shorten thy life one weeke .

4   And thou, fresh peece
    Of excellent Witchcraft, [whom] of force must know
    The royall Foole thou coap'st with .

---

5   Ile have thy beauty scratcht with briers & made
    More homely [then] thy state .

6   For thee(fond boy)
    If I may ever know thou dost but sigh,
    That thou no more shalt [never] see this knacke (as never
    I meane thou shalt) wee'l barre thee from succession,
    Not hold thee of our blood, no not our Kin,
    Farre [then] Deucalion off :(marke thou my words)
    Follow us to the Court .

7   Thou Churle, for this time
    (Though full of our displeasure) yet we free thee
    From the dead blow of it .

8   And you Enchantment,
    Worthy enough a Heardsman : yea him too,
    That makes himselfe (but for our Honor therein)
    Unworthy thee .

9   If ever henceforth, thou
    These rurall Latches, to his entrance open,
    Or [hope] his body more, with thy embraces,
    I will devise a death, as cruell for thee
    As thou art tender to't .

- the opening series of attacks on each of them (F #1-4) is emotional (4/10 in the first eight lines of the speech)
- the second round of attacks on Perdita and then Florizell is unembellished (F #5 and the first two and half lines of F #6), suggesting that Polixines controls his anger, at least for four lines, but he then explodes emotionally once more as he threatens Florizell that he will 'barre thee from succession' (3/6, the last four lines of F #6)
- the second attack on her father and then the start of the third attack on Perdita, are both passionate (4/3, F #7-8), and though the words of his final threat to Perdita are very real (F #9), the extra breath-thoughts (marked ,) and the relative lack of release (1/2 in four lines) suggest that it appears he is trying to re-establish some form of self-control
- the icy unembellished attacks on his son start with the statement that he is
  "too base/To be acknowledged."
  followed later with
  "For thee (fond boy)/If I may ever know thou dost but sigh,/That thou no more shalt never see this…"
- and though the initial attack on Perdita's father leaves no room for doubt, the last word 'weeke' the only thing to break the quietness
  "I am sorry, that by hanging thee, I can/But shorten thy life one weeke"
  Polixines soon softens towards him, if only a little
  "(Though full of our displeasure) yet we free thee/From the dead blow of it"
- while the attack on Perdita is very clear
  "Ile have thy beauty scratcht with briers & made/More homely then thy state."
  warning her later that should she
  "to his entrance open, or [hope] his body more, with thy embraces,/I will devise a death,…"

The Winter's Tale

Leontes

Her naturall Posture .
between 5.3.23–73

Background: Leontes first response to the sight of Hermione as 'statue', even before Paulina brings 'it' to 'life'.

Style: as part of a four-handed scene in front of a larger group

Where: in Paulina's art gallery

To Whom: the statue, Paulina and Polixines, in front of the larger group comprising Camillo, Perdita, Florizell, and accompanying Lords and Musicians

# of Lines: 20

Probable Timing: 1.00 minutes

Take Note: The confusion in Leontes is seen not merely in the contradictory request of F #2, but also in the opening orthography—for the shortness of F #1, the three surround phrases completely forming F #2, and F #2's two extra breath-thoughts (marked ,) all speak to a mind having difficulty in coping. Thus it's also interesting to note that proportionately there are far more releases in the first fourteen lines (21/11) up to and including the order 'Doe not draw the Curtaine', than in the last six (4/4), when he is assured that he can gaze his fill.

Leontes

1   Her natural posture !

2   Chide me, dear stone, that I may say indeed
    Thou art Hermione ; or rather, thou art she
    In thy not chiding ; for she was as tender
    As infancy and grace .

---

3   O, thus she stood,
    Even with such life of majesty (warm life,
    As now it coldly stands), when first I woo'd her !

4   I am asham'd ; does not the stone rebuke me
    For being more stone [than] it ?

5   O royal piece,
    There's magic in thy majesty, which has
    My evils conjur'd to remembrance, and
    From thy admiring daughter took the spirits,
    Standing like stone with thee .

---

6   Do not draw the Curtain .

---

7   Let be, let be .

8   Would I were dead, but that [methinks] already -
    (What was he that did make it ?)

9   See, my lord,
    Would you not deem it breath'd ? and that those veins
    Did verily bear blood ?

---

10 The [fixture] of her eye has motion in't,
    As we are mock'd with art .

---

11   Let't alone .

Leontes

1 Her naturall Posture .

2 Chide me(deare Stone) that I may say indeed
   Thou art Hermione ; or rather, thou art she,
   In thy not chiding : for she was as tender
   As Infancie, and Grace .

3   Oh, thus she stood,
   Even with such Life of Majestie (warme Life,
   As now it coldly stands) when first I woo'd her .

4 I am asham'd : Do's not the Stone rebuke me,
   For being more Stone [then] it ?

5   Oh Royall Peece :
   There's Magick in thy Majestie, which ha's
   My Evils conjur'd to remembrance ; and
   From thy admiring Daughter tooke the Spirits,
   Standing like Stone with thee .

6 Doe not draw the Curtaine .

7 Let be, let be :
   Would I were dead, but that [me thinkes]alreadie .

8 (What was he that did make it ?)

9   See(my Lord)
   Would you not deeme it breath'd ? and that those veines
   Did verily beare blood ?

10 The [fixure] of her Eye ha's motion in't,
    As we are mock'd with Art .

11   Let't alone .

- even so, the speech starts highly intellectually(13/3, F 1-4), suggesting a certainty of both how closely the statue resembles his memory of Hermione, and of his own guilt—the latter underscored by the unembellished surround phrase opening F #4, ' . I am asham'd : '

- framing F #5's praise to the 'Magicke in thy Majestie' come two of only three emotional clusters in the speech, the opening 'Oh Royall Peece' (2/3 in three words!), and the short sentence plea of F #6's 'Doe not draw the Curtaine.' (1/2)

- with the 'Curtaine' staying open, so Leontes begins to quieten, his ironic comment about him in essence being dead almost unembellished (0/1, F #7, suggesting that quite a truth has been uttered), followed by the unembellished request to know the sculptor's identity (F #8)

- as Leontes becomes aware of the others accompanying him for, it would seem, the first time in the speech, he becomes emotional in asking at least one of them (probably Polixenes) to comment upon the life-like quality of the 'statue' (1/3), while his adding his own proof via the 'fixure of her Eye' becomes intellectual once more

- and in the last moment of the speech he seems wrapped in wonder, with F #11's incredibly short unembellished 'Let't alone' being all he can finally say

The Tempest

Gonzalo

Had I plantation of this Isle my Lord,
between 2.1.144–168

Background: described by Prospero both as a 'Noble Neopolitan' and 'Holy Gonzalo', Gonzalo is doing anything he can to bring Alonso, the King of Naples, distraught at the apparent drowning death of his son Ferdinand, back into a sense of current reality and responsibility so as to unite the increasingly bickering fragmented group (the two factions being the darker forces of Anthonio and Sebastian on the one hand, and the leaderless remainder, including 'good' Gonzalo, on the other).

Style: one on one address in front of a larger group

Where: unspecified, somewhere on the island

To Whom: Alonso, in front of Sebastian, Anthonio, Adrian and Francisco, and an unspecified number of 'others'

# of Lines: 19

Probable Timing: 1.00 minutes

Take Note: This sequence is often played as one long boring blab, yet F's orthography clearly shows a key difference in conception and realisation between (the discoveries of?) F #2 and (the resultant reverie of F #3).

Gonzalo

1   Had I plantation of this isle my lord—

And were the king on't, what would I do ?

---

2   I'th' commonwealth I would, by contraries,
    Execute all things ; for no kind of traffic
    Would I admit ; no name of magistrate ;
    Letters should not be known; riches, poverty,
    And use of service, none ; contract, succession,
    [Bourn], bound of land, tilth, vineyard none ;
    No use of metal, corn, or wine, or oil;
    No occupation, all men idle, all ;
    And women too, but innocent and pure ;
    No soveraignty—

All things in common nature should produce
Without sweat or endeavor : treason, felony,
Sword, pike, knife, gun, or need of any engine,
Would I not have ; but nature should bring forth,
Of it own kind, all foison, all abundance,
To feed my innocent people .

---

3   I would with such perfection govern, Sir,
    T'excel the golden age .

Gonzalo

1   Had I plantation of this Isle my Lord {,}

And were the King on't, what would I do ?

2   I'th'Commonwealth I would (by contraries)
Execute all things : For no kinde of Trafficke
Would I admit : No name of Magistrate :
Letters should not be knowne : Riches, poverty,
And use of service, none : Contract, Succession,
[Borne], bound of Land, Tilth, Vineyard none :
No use of Mettall, Corne, or Wine, or Oyle :
No occupation, all men idle, all :
And Women too, but innocent and pure :
No Soveraignty .

3   All things in common Nature should produce
Without sweat or endevour : Treason, fellony,
Sword, Pike, Knife, Gun, or neede of any Engine
Would I not have : but Nature should bring forth
Of it owne kinde, all foyzon, all abundance
To feed my innocent people .

4   I would with such perfection governe Sir :
T'Excell the Golden Age .

- In trying to get Alonso's attention, Gonzalo opens quite intellectually (4/0, F #1 and the first line and half of F #2), but once the idea of ruling by 'contraries' is voiced, so his pattern completely changes.

- The lengthy F #2 itemising how this would work is composed entirely of ten surround phrases, and whether this is an attempt to get through to the distracted Alonso, or is indicative of his own mind running rampant with the somewhat revolutionary ideas (though modern editors suggest that this passage is meant as a criticism of the rather startling propositions of the French philosopher Montaigne) is up to each actor to decide.

- The first explorations in the denial-of-status-distinction ideas from 'For no kinde of Trafficke/Would I admit' through to 'And use of service, none', is passionate (4/3 in just three lines), and then moving into concerns of business and the impact of the new order on human beings becomes intellectual (11/3, the last five lines of F #2).

- And with F #3's utopian overview, the surround phrases, if such still can be said to exist, become much longer, and though the suggestion that 'Nature' should be allowed to develop without 'sweat or endevour' still remains intellectual (6/3, the first three and half lines of F #3), the shift into the idealistic hope that 'Nature should bring forth/ Of it owne kinde' becomes (delightedly?) emotional (1/3).

- F #4's intellectual, surpassing the 'Golden Age', finale (4/2) is heightened by being expressed once again via two surround phrases.

The Tempest

Prospero

Ye Elves of hils, brooks, stãding lakes & groves,
5.1.33–57

Background: though his former enemies are in his power, Prospero still has to meet them face to face, and, judging by the enormous power of which he boasts in the following speech, and Miranda's concern as expressed earlier to Ferdinand 'Never till this day/Saw I him touch'd with anger, so distemper'd', he has not yet resolved whether to free or destroy them. Here, he is gathering his strength for this, as he judges it, his final major task.

Style: ostensibly solo, yet directed towards a series of highly detailed personal visions

Where: unspecified, but somewhere close to his cell

To Whom: all the spirits from which he draws his power

# of Lines: 25

Probable Timing: 1.15 minutes

Take Note: In this speech the releases often seem more attached to specific images rather than a concentrated passage of one particular form of release: apart from single releases scattered throughout there are occasional clusters, which would include

  a. intellectually, the 'Noone-tide Sun'; 'Joves stowt Oke'; the 'Pyne and Cedar'
  b. emotionally, with 'printlesse foote/Doe chase'; 'that rejoyce/To heare the solemne Curfewe'; 'this rough Magicke/I heere abjure'; 'I'le breake my staffe'; 'Ile drowne my booke'

Prospero

1   Ye elves of hills, brooks, [standing] lakes, & groves,
    And ye that on the sands with printless foot
    Do chase the ebbing Neptune, and do fly him
    When he comes back ; you demi-puppets that
    By moon shine do the green sour ringlets make,
    Whereof the ewe not bites ; and you whose pastime
    Is to make midnight mushrumps, that rejoice
    To hear the solemn curfew: by whose aid
    (Weak masters though ye be) I have bedimm'd
    The noon tide sun, call'd forth the mutinous winds,
    And 'twixt the green sea and the azur'd vault
    Set roaring war; to the dread rattling thunder
    Have I given fire, and rifted Jove's stout oak
    With his own bolt ; the strong bass'd promontory
    Have I made shake, and by the spurs pluck'd up
    The pine and cedar .

2   **Graves at my command**
    Have wak'd their sleepers, op'd, and let 'em forth
    By my so potent art .

3   But this rough magic
    I here abjure ; and when I have requir'd
    Some heavenly Music (which even now I do)
    To work mine end upon their senses that
    This airy charm is for, I'll break my staff,
    Bury it certain [fathoms] in the earth,
    And deeper [than] did ever plummet sound
    I'll drown my book .

Prospero

1   Ye Elves of hils, brooks, [stãding] lakes & groves,
And ye, that on the sands with printlesse foote
Doe chase the ebbing-Neptune, and doe flie him
When he comes backe : you demy-Puppets, that
By Moone-shine doe the greene sowre Ringlets make,
Whereof the Ewe not bites : and you, whose pastime
Is to make midnight-Mushrumps, that rejoyce
To heare the solemne Curfewe, by whose ayde
(Weake Masters though ye be) I have bedymn'd
The Noone-tide Sun, call'd forth the mutenous windes,
And twixt the greene Sea, and the azur'd vault
Set roaring warre : To the dread ratling Thunder
Have I given fire, and rifted Joves stowt Oke
With his owne Bolt : The strong bass'd promontorie
Have I made shake, and by the spurs pluckt up
The Pyne, and Cedar .

2   **Graves at my command
Have wak'd their sleepers,** op'd and let 'em forth
By my so potent Art .

3   But this rough Magicke
I heere abjure : and when I have requir'd
Some heavenly Musicke (which even now I do)
To worke mine end upon their Sences, that
This Ayrie-charme is for, I'le breake my staffe,
Bury it certaine [fadomes] in the earth,
And deeper [then] did ever Plummet sound
Ile drowne my booke .

- Prospero's opening appeal to the 'Elves' is emotional (2/5, the first three and a half lines); and then he becomes passionate as he next calls upon the 'demy-Puppets' (4/3), and those 'whose pastime /Is to make midnight-Mushrumps' (2/4), in which vein he stays as he recalls how he has striven with nature—the 'Noone-tide Sun', the 'mutenous windes', the 'greene Sea' (4/7)

- but, as he recalls challenging Jove, and uprooting trees, and even opening graves, so his intellect begins to assert itself (8/3), though interestingly each image declines in intensity, from the powerful surround phrase of

    a. " . To the dread ratling Thunder/Have I given fire, and rifted Joves stowt Oke/With his owne Bolt : " (5/2)

    b. through to the uprooting of trees (3/1)

    c. to the almost hushed two line F #2 image of graves letting forth their sleepers (1/0), suggesting either diminishing energy (see the previous speech) or that he becomes quieter as he realises the enormity of what he dared to achieve—yet the magical pattern of the (bolded) opening (see Appendix 3 for a more detailed explanation of the patterns of magic) suggests an enormous sense of power (and even danger?) within the recollection—the calm perhaps suggesting that he is struggling to contain the enormously dangerous thoughts the image triggers/contains

- thus the enormity of the vow that opens F #3 is doubly enhanced, first by being set as a surround phrase

    " . But this rough Magicke/I heere abjure : "

and in turn by being part of a highly emotional sentence (5/11) containing both his quest for 'Some heavenly Musicke' to achieve what must be done with Alonso, Sebastian, and above all brother Anthonio, and his promise to 'breake my staffe' and 'drowne my booke', i.e to end his magical powers once and for all

BIBLIOGRAPHY

AND

APPENDICES

BIBLIOGRAPHY

The most easily accessible general information is to be found under the citations of *Campbell,* and of *Halliday.* The finest summation of matters academic is to be found within the all-encompassing *A Textual Companion,* listed below in the first part of the bibliography under *Wells, Stanley and Taylor, Gary* (eds.)

Individual modern editions consulted are listed below under the separate headings 'The Complete Works in Compendium Format' and 'The Complete Works in Separate Individual Volumes,' from which the modern text audition speeches have been collated and compiled.

All modern act, scene, and/or line numbers refer the reader to *The Riverside Shakespeare,* in my opinion still the best of the complete works, despite the excellent compendiums that have been published since.

The F/Q material is taken from a variety of already published sources, including not only all the texts listed in the 'Photostatted Reproductions in Compendium Format' below, but also earlier individually printed volumes, such as the twentieth century editions published under the collective title *The Facsimiles of Plays from The First Folio of Shakespeare* by Faber & Gwyer, and the nineteenth century editions published on behalf of The New Shakespere Society.

The heading 'Single Volumes of Special Interest' is offered to newcomers to Shakespeare in the hope that the books may add useful knowledge about the background and craft of this most fascinating of theatrical figures.

PHOTOSTATTED REPRODUCTIONS OF THE ORIGINAL TEXTS IN COMPENDIUM FORMAT

Allen, M.J.B. and K. Muir, (eds.). *Shakespeare's Plays in Quarto.* Berkeley: University of California Press, 1981.

Blaney, Peter (ed.). *The Norton Facsimile (The First Folio of Shakespeare).* New York: W.W.Norton & Co., Inc., 1996 (see also Hinman, below).

Brewer D.S. (ed.). *Mr. William Shakespeare's Comedies, Histories & Tragedies, The Second/Third/Fourth Folio Reproduced in Facsimile.* (3 vols.), 1983.

Hinman, Charlton (ed.). *The Norton Facsimile (The First Folio of Shakespeare)*. New York: W.W.Norton & Company, Inc., 1968.

Kokeritz, Helge (ed.). *Mr. William Shakespeare 's Comedies, Histories & Tragedies.* New Haven: Yale University Press, 1954.

Moston, Doug (ed.). *Mr. William Shakespeare's Comedies, Histories, and Tragedies.* New York: Routledge, 1998.

MODERN TYPE VERSION OF THE FIRST FOLIO IN COMPENDIUM FORMAT

Freeman, Neil. (ed.). *The Applause First Folio of Shakespeare in Modern Type.* New York & London: Applause Books, 2001.

MODERN TEXT VERSIONS OF THE COMPLETE WORKS IN COMPENDIUM FORMAT

Craig, H. and D. Bevington (eds.). *The Complete Works of Shakespeare.* Glenview: Scott, Foresman and Company, 1973.

Evans, G.B. (ed.). *The Riverside Shakespeare.* Boston: Houghton Mifflin Company, 1974.

Wells, Stanley and Gary Taylor (eds.). *The Oxford Shakespeare, William Shakespeare , the Complete Works, Original Spelling Edition,* Oxford: The Clarendon Press, 1986.

Wells, Stanley and Gary Taylor (eds.). *The Oxford Shakespeare, William Shakespeare, The Complete Works, Modern Spelling Edition.* Oxford: The Clarendon Press, 1986.

MODERN TEXT VERSIONS OF THE COMPLETE WORKS IN SEPARATE INDIVIDUAL VOLUMES

The Arden Shakespeare. London: Methuen & Co. Ltd., Various dates, editions, and editors .

Folio Texts. Freeman, Neil H. M. (ed.) Applause First Folio Editions, 1997, and following.

The New Cambridge Shakespeare. Cambridge: Cambridge University Press. Various dates, editions, and editors.

New Variorum Editions of Shakespeare. Furness, Horace Howard (original editor.). New York: 1880, Various reprints. All these volumes have been in a state of re-editing and reprinting since they first appeared in 1880. Various dates, editions, and editors.

The Oxford Shakespeare. Wells, Stanley (general editor). Oxford: Oxford University Press, Various dates and editors.

The New Penguin Shakespeare . Harmondsworth, Middlesex: Penguin Books, Various dates and editors.

The Shakespeare Globe Acting Edition. Tucker, Patrick and Holden, Michael. (eds.). London: M.H.Publications, Various dates.

SINGLE VOLUMES OF SPECIAL INTEREST

Baldwin, T.W. *William Shakespeare's Petty School.* 1943.

Baldwin, T.W. *William Shakespeare's Small wtin and Lesse Greeke.* (2 vols.) 1944.

Barton, John. *Playing Shakespeare.* 1984.

Beckerman, Bernard. *Shakespeare at the Globe, I 599-1609.* 1962. Berryman, John. *Berryman 's Shakespeare.* 1999.

Bloom, Harold. *Shakespeare: The Invention of the Human.* 1998. Booth, Stephen (ed.). *Shakespeare's Sonnets.* 1977.

Briggs, Katharine. *An Encyclopedia of Fairies.* 1976.

Campbell, Oscar James, and Edward G. Quinn (eds.). *The Reader's Encyclopedia of Shakespeare. 1966.*

Crystal, David, and Ben Crystal. *Shakespeare's Words: A Glossary & Language Companion.* 2002.

Flatter, Richard. *Shakespeare's Producing Hand.* 1948 (reprint).

Ford, Boris. (ed.). *The Age of Shakespeare.* 1955.

Freeman, Neil H.M. *Shakespeare's First Texts.* 1994.

Greg, W.W. *The Editorial Problem in Shakespeare: A Survey of the Foundations of the Text.* 1954 (3rd. edition).

Gurr, Andrew . *Playgoing in Shakespeare's London.* 1987. Gurr, Andrew. *The Shakespearean Stage, 1574-1642.* 1987. Halliday, F.E. *A Shakespeare Companion.* 1952.

Harbage, Alfred. *Shakespeare's Audience.* 1941.

Harrison, G.B. (ed.). *The Elizabethan Journals.* 1965 (revised, 2 vols.).

Harrison, G.B. (ed.). *A Jacobean Journal.* 1941.

Harrison, G.B. (ed.). *A Second Jacobean Journal.* 1958.

Hinman, Charlton. *The Printing and Proof Reading of the First Folio of Shakespeare.* 1963 (2 vols.).

Joseph, Bertram. *Acting Shakespeare.* 1960.

Joseph, Miriam (Sister). *Shakespeare's Use of The Arts of wnguage.*1947.

King, T.J. *Casting Shakespeare's Plays.* 1992.

Lee, Sidney and C.T. Onions. *Shakespeare's England : An Account Of The Life And Manners Of His Age.* (2 vols.) 1916.

Linklater, Kristin. *Freeing Shakespeare's Voice*. 1992.

Mahood, **M .M**. *Shakespeare's Wordplay*. 1957.

O'Connor, Gary. *William Shakespeare: A Popular Life*. 2000.

Ordish, T.F. *Early London Theatres*. 1894. (1971 reprint).

Rodenberg, Patsy. *Speaking Shakespeare*. 2002.

Schoenbaum. S. *William Shakespeare: A Documentary Life*. 1975.

Shapiro, Michael. *Children of the Revels*. 1977.

Simpson, Percy. *Shakespeare's Punctuation*. 1969 (reprint).

Smith, Irwin. *Shakespeare's Blackfriars Playhouse* . 1964.

Southern, Richard. *The Staging of Plays Before Shakespeare*. 1973.

Spevack, M. *A Complete and Systematic Concordance to the Works Of Shakespeare* . 1968-1980 (9vols.).

Tillyard, E.M.W. *The Elizabethan World Picture*. 1942.

Trevelyan, G.M. (ed.). *Illustrated English Social History*. 1942.

Vendler, Helen. *The Art of Shakespeare's Sonnets*. 1999.

Walker, Alice F. *Textual Problems of the First Folio*. 1953.

Walton, J.K. *The Quarto Copy of the First Folio*. 1971.

Warren, Michael. *William Shakespeare, The Parallel King Lear 1608-1623*.

Wells, Stanley and Taylor, Gary (eds.). *Modernising Shakespeare's Spelling, with Three Studies in The Text of Henry V.* 1975.

Wells, Stanley. *Re-Editing Shakespeare for the Modern Reader.* 1984.

Wells, Stanley and Gary Taylor (eds.). *William Shakespeare: A Textual Companion* . 1987.

Wright, George T. *Shakespeare's Metrical Art*. 1988.

HISTORICAL DOCUMENTS

Daniel, Samuel. *The Fowre Bookes of the Civile Warres Between The Howses Of Lancaster and Yorke.* 1595.

Holinshed, Raphael. *Chronicles of England, Scotland and Ireland.* 1587 (2nd. edition).

Halle, Edward. *The Union of the Two Noble and Illustre Famelies of Lancastre And Yorke.* 1548 (2nd. edition).

Henslowe, Philip: Foakes, R.A. and Rickert (eds.). *Henslowe's Diary.* 1961.

Plutarch: North, Sir Thomas (translation of a work in French prepared by Jacques Amyots). *The Lives of The Noble Grecians and Romanes.* 1579.

APPENDIX 1:
GUIDE TO THE EARLY TEXTS

A QUARTO (Q)

A single text, so called because of the book size resulting from a particular method of printing. Eighteen of Shakespeare's plays were published in this format by different publishers at various dates between 1594-1622, prior to the appearance of the 1623 Folio.

THE FIRST FOLIO (F1)'

Thirty-six of Shakespeare's plays (excluding *Pericles* and *Two Noble Kinsmen,* in which he had a hand) appeared in one volume, published in 1623. All books of this size were termed Folios, again because of the sheet size and printing method, hence this volume is referred to as the First Folio. For publishing details see Bibliography, 'Photostated Reproductions of the Original Texts.'

THE SECOND FOLIO (F2)

Scholars suggest that the Second Folio, dated 1632 but perhaps not published until 1640, has little authority, especially since it created hundreds of new problematic readings of its own. Nevertheless more than 800 modern text readings can be attributed to it. The **Third Folio** (1664) and the **Fourth Folio** (1685) have even less authority, and are rarely consulted except in cases of extreme difficulty.

APPENDIX 2:
WORD, WORDS, WORDS

PART ONE: VERBAL CONVENTIONS (AND HOW THEY WILL BE SET IN THE FOLIO TEXT)

"THEN" AND "THAN"

These two words, though their neutral vowels sound different to modern ears, were almost identical to Elizabethan speakers and readers, despite their different meanings. F and Q make little distinction between them, setting them interchangeably . The original setting will be used, and the modern reader should soon get used to substituting one for the other as necessary.

"I," "AY," AND "AYE"

F/Q often print the personal pronoun "I" and the word of agreement "aye" simply as "I." Again, the modern reader should quickly get used to this and make the substitution when necess ary. The reader should also be aware that very occasionally either word could be used and the phrase make perfect sense, even though different meanings would be implied.

"MY SELFE/HIM SELFE/HER SELFE" VERSUS "MYSELF/HIMSELF/HERSELF"

Generally F/Q separate the two parts of the word, "my selfe" while most modern texts set the single word "myself." The difference is vital, based on Elizabethan philosophy. Elizabethans regarded themselves as composed of two parts, the corporeal "I," and the more spiritual part, the "self." Thus, when an Elizabethan character refers to "my selfe," he or she is often referring to what is to all intents and purposes a separate being, even if that being is a particular part of him- or herself. Thus soliloquies can be thought of as a debate between the "I" and "my selfe," and, in such speeches, even though there may be only one character on-stage, it's as if there were two distinct entities present.

UNUSUAL SPELLING OF REAL NAMES, BOTH OF PEOPLE AND PLACES

Real names, both of people and places, and foreign languages are often reworked for modern understanding. For example, the French town often set in Fl as "Callice" is usually reset as "Calais." F will be set as is.

NON-GRAMMATICAL USES OF VERBS IN BOTH TENSE AND APPLICATION

Modern texts 'correct' the occasional Elizabethan practice of setting a singular noun with plural verb (and vice versa), as well as the infrequent use of the past tense of a verb to describe a current situation. The F reading will be set as is, without annotation.

ALTERNATIVE SETTINGS OF A WORD WHERE DIFFERENT SPELLINGS MAINTAIN THE SAME MEANING

F/Q occasionally set what appears to modern eyes as an archaic spelling of a word for which there is a more common modern alternative, for example "murther" for murder , "burthen" for burden, "moe" for more, "vilde" for vile. Though some modern texts set the Fl (or alternative Q) setting, others modernise. Fl will be set as is with no annotation.

ALTERNATIVE SETTINGS OF A WORD WHERE DIFFERENT SPELLINGS SUGGEST DIFFERENT MEANINGS

Far more complicated is the situation where, while an Elizabethan could substitute one word formation for another and still imply the same thing, to modern eyes the substituted word has an entirely different meaning to the one it has replaced. The following is by no means an exclusive list of the more common dual-spelling, dual-meaning words

anticke-antique	mad-made	sprite-spirit
born-borne	metal-mettle	sun-sonne
hart-heart	mote-moth	travel-travaill
human-humane	pour-(po wre)-power	through-thorough
lest-least	reverent-reverend	troth-truth
lose-loose	right-rite	whether-whither

Some of these doubles offer a metrical problem too, for example "sprite," a one syllable word, versus "spirit." A potential problem occurs in *A Midsummer Nights Dream,* where the modern text s set Q1's "thorough," and thus the scansion pattern of elegant magic can be established, whereas F1's more plebeian "through" sets up a much more awkward and clumsy moment.

The F reading will be set in the Folio Text, as will the modern texts' substitution of a different word formation in the Modern Text. If the modern text substitution has the potential to alter the meaning (and sometimes scansion) of the line, it will be noted accordingly.

PART TWO: WORD FORMATIONS COUNTED AS EQUIVALENTS FOR THE FOLLOWING SPEECHES

Often the spelling differences between the original and modern texts are quite obvious, as with "she"/"shee". And sometimes Folio text passages are so flooded with longer (and sometimes shorter) spellings that, as described in the General Introduction, it would seem that vocally something unusual is taking place as the character speaks.

However, there are some words where the spelling differences are so marginal that they need not be explored any further. The following is by no mean s an exclusive list of word s that in the main will not be taken into account when discussing emotional moments in the various commentaries accompanying the audition speeches.

(modern text spelling shown first)

and- &	murder - murther	tabor - taber
apparent - apparant	mutinous - mutenous	ta'en - tane
briars - briers	naught - nought	then - than
choice - choise	obey - obay	theater - theatre
defense - defence	o'er - o're	uncurrant - uncurrent
debtor - debter	offense - offence	than - then
enchant - inchant	quaint - queint	venomous - venemous
endurance - indurance	reside - recide	virtue - vertue
ere - e'er	Saint - S.	weight - waight
expense - expence	sense - sence	
has - ha's	sepulchre - sepulcher	
heinous - hainous	show - shew	
I'll - Ile	solicitor - soliciter	
increase - encrease	sugar - suger	

APPENDIX 3:
THE PATTERN OF MAGIC, RITUAL &
INCANTATION

THE PATTERNS OF "NORMAL" CONVERSATION

The normal pattern of a regular Shakespearean verse line is akin to five pairs of human heart beats, with ten syllables being arranged in five pairs of beats, each pair alternating a pattern of a weak stress followed by a strong stress. Thus, a normal ten syllable heartbeat line (with the emphasis on the capitalised words) would read as

weak- STRONG, weak - STRONG, weak- STRONG, weak- STRONG, weak- STRONG
(shall I   com-   PARE thee TO   a   SUMM- ers DAY)

Breaks would either be in length (under or over ten syllables) or in rhythm (any combinations of stresses other than the five pairs of weak-strong as shown above), or both together.

THE PATTERNS OF MAGIC, RITUAL, AND INCANTATION

Whenever magic is used in the Shakespeare plays the form of the spoken verse changes markedly in two ways . The length is usually reduced from ten to just seven syllables, and the pattern of stresses is completely reversed, as if the heartbeat was being forced either by the circumstances of the scene or by the need of the speaker to completely change direction. Thus in comparison to the normal line shown above, or even the occasional minor break, the more tortured and even dangerous magic or ritual line would read as

STRONG - weak, STRONG- weak, STRONG - weak, STRONG
(WHEN   shall   WE   three   MEET   a   GAINE)

The strain would be even more severely felt in an extended passage, as when the three weyward Sisters begin the potion that will fetch Macbeth to them. Again, the spoken emphasis is on the capitalised words and the effort of, and/or fixed determination in, speaking can clearly be felt.

> THRICE the BRINDed CAT hath MEW"D
> THRICE and ONCE the HEDGE-Pigge WHIN"D
> HARPier CRIES, 'tis TIME, 'tis TIME.

UNUSUAL ASPECTS OF MAGIC

It's not always easy for the characters to maintain it. And the magic doesn't always come when the character expects it. What is even more interesting is that while the pattern is found a lot in the Comedies, it is usually in much gentler situations, often in songs *(Two Gentlemen of Verona, Merry Wives of Windsor, Much Ado About Nothing, Twelfth Night, The Winters Tale)* and/or simplistic poetry *(Loves Labours Lost* and *As You Like It),* as well as the casket sequence in *The Merchant of Venice.*

It's too easy to dismiss these settings as inferior poetry known as doggerel. But this may be doing the moment and the character a great disservice. The language may be simplistic, but the passion and the magical/ritual intent behind it is wonderfully sincere. It's not just a matter of magic for the sake of magic, as with Pucke and Oberon enchanting mortals and Titania. It's a matter of the human heart's desires too. Orlando, in *As You Like It,* when writing peons of praise to Rosalind suggesting that she is composed of the best parts of the mythical heroines because

> THEREfore HEAVen NATure CHARG"D
> THAT one BODie SHOULD be FILL"D
> WITH all GRACes WIDE enLARG"D

And what could be better than Autolycus *(The Winters Tale)* using magic in his opening song as an extra enticement to trap the unwary into buying all his peddler's goods, ballads, and trinkets.

To help the reader, most magic/ritual lines will be bolded in the Folio text version of the speeches.

ACKNOWLEDGMENTS

Neil dedicated *The Applause First Folio in Modern Type*
"To All Who Have Gone Before"
and there are so many who have gone before in the sharing of Shakespeare through publication. Back to John Heminge and Henry Condell who published *Mr. William Shakespeares Comedies, Histories, & Tragedies* which we now know as The First Folio and so preserved 18 plays of Shakespeare which might otherwise have been lost. As they wrote in their note "To the great Variety of Readers.":

> Reade him, therefore; and againe, and againe : And if then you doe not like him, surely you are in some manifest danger, not to understand him. And so we leave you to other of his Friends, whom if you need, can be your guides: if you neede them not, you can lead yourselves, and others, and such readers we wish him.

I want to thank John Cerullo for believing in these books and helping to spread Neil's vision. I want to thank Rachel Reiss for her invaluable advice and assistance. I want to thank my wife, Maren and my family for giving me support, but above all I want to thank Julie Stockton, Neil's widow, who was able to retrive Neil's files from his old non-internet connected Mac, without which these books would not be possible. Thank you Julie.

Shakespeare for Everyone!

Paul Sugarman, April 2021

AUTHOR BIOS

Neil Freeman (1941-2015) trained as an actor at the Bristol Old Vic Theatre School. In the world of professional Shakespeare he acted in fourteen of the plays, directed twenty-four, and coached them all many times over.

His groundbreaking work in using the first printings of the Shakespeare texts in performance, on the rehearsal floor and in the classroom led to lectures at the Shakespeare Association of America and workshops at both the ATHE and VASTA, and grants/fellowships from the National Endowment for the Arts (USA), The Social Science and Humanities Research Council (Canada), and York University in Toronto. He prepared and annotated the thirty-six individual Applause First Folio editions of Shakespeare's plays and the complete *The Applause First Folio of Shakespeare in Modern Type*. For Applause he also compiled *Once More Unto the Speech, Dear Friends*, three volumes (Comedy, History and Tragedy) of Shakespeare speeches with commentary and insights to inform audition preparation.

He was Professor Emeritus in the Department of Theatre, Film and Creative Writing at the University of British Columbia, and dramaturg with The Savage God project, both in Vancouver, Canada. He also taught regularly at the National Theatre School of Canada, Concordia University, Brigham Young University.. He had a Founder's Ring (and the position of Master Teacher) with Shakespeare & Company in Lenox, Mass: he was associated with the Will Geer Theatre in Los Angeles; Bard on the Beach in Vancouver; Repercussion Theatre in Montreal; and worked with the Stratford Festival, Canada, and Shakespeare Santa Cruz.

Paul Sugarman is an actor, editor, writer, and teacher of Shakespeare. He is founder of the Instant Shakespeare Company, which has presented annual readings of all of Shakespeare's plays in New York City for over twenty years. For Applause Theatre & Cinema Books, he edited John Russell Brown's publication of *Shakescenes: Shakespeare for Two* and The Applause Shakespeare Library, as well as Neil Freeman's Applause First Folio Editions and *The Applause First Folio of Shakespeare in Modern Type*. He has published pocket editions of all of Shakespeare's plays using the original settings of the First Folio in modern type for Puck Press. Sugarman studied with Kristin Linklater and Tina Packer at Shakespeare & Company where he met Neil Freeman.